The

Enterprise

Data Model

A framework for enterprise data architecture, Second Edition

By Andy Graham

Published by Koios Associates Ltd

Printed in the United States of America.

Table of Contents

Contents

Contents

Table of Figures

Table of Figures

Preface

Wouldn't it be great to understand all the data in your organisation? Just imagine being able to define, agree and manage information concepts that impact on business strategy? Then imagine that these information concepts can be linked to the physical database attributes that ultimately are used to create them. That's what this book is about. It focuses on the data model as the foundation for achieving this understanding

Let's be candid, most organisations struggle to find a way to control the data whirlwind that has hit them over the last few decades. This book attempts to re-address some of the balance.

My inspiration has been the numerous requests I've received from clients to understand the meaning of an enterprise data model, and how to use this concept successfully. This approach and resulting framework has been developed over many years through the trials and tribulations of numerous data related projects. The clients I've worked with span right across the spectrum from financial services, utility, exploration, government to FMCG. This framework is universal in its application as are many (if not most) of the challenges associated with data.

In the normal course of events I would spend many hours discussing data architecture and modelling with the client, to evolve an approach which is suitable for their particular organisation. Often I've written client specific papers on this subject or pulled together presentations that explain the concepts. This book is an attempt to capture this knowledge so that a wider audience can take advantage of it. I have described the salient points and provided a generic framework which can be tailored to fit the readers own organisation.

The intended audience of this text include data professionals, managers of data professionals, project/program managers, IT architects of all kinds and business analysts. There are also a number of chapters, specifically the introduction and business justification, which will be of interest to the executive levels within an organisation.

This book covers a range of subjects all of which are impacted by the enterprise data model. There are 11 chapters and 2 appendices:

- **Chapter 1 – Introduction**: The book starts with a general overview of the purpose and history of the data model.
- **Chapter 2 – Information and Data:** We next look at the difference between information and data. Although on first glance this may seem an obvious difference, experience says that confusion can sometimes occur.
- **Chapter 3 – Pillars of Value:** In this chapter we address the business justification that supports the enterprise data model.
- **Chapter 4 – An Overview of Data Modelling:** This chapter is a basic introduction to data modelling. It has been included to provide some background to the rest of the book. This chapter is NOT a detailed look at the process and techniques involved in designing a data model just a quick overview and nothing more.

- **Chapter 5 – Enterprise Data Architecture:** Introduces a basic data architecture framework; with a look at the elements of data architecture that rely upon an enterprise data model to function.
- **Chapter 6 – The Enterprise Data Model:** This chapter gets to the heart of the subject matter and explains the different types of models and how they all interact.
- **Chapter 7 – Needs and Process:** This chapter looks at how we can map processes, data flows and business requirements to the enterprise data model.
- **Chapter 8 – Master Your Data:** A chapter on Master Data Management is included as there is a huge degree of overlap between these two subject areas.
- **Chapter 9 – Data Governance:** We look at the value brought to the data governance process by an enterprise data model. A look at how this can aid dealing with outsourced service providers is also touched upon.
- **Chapter 10 – Build the Model one Project at a Time:** With this chapter we examine some of the practicalities of actually building an enterprise data model so that it doesn't become a massive white elephant project.
- **Chapter 11 – The Enterprise Data Framework:** The final chapter summaries the enterprise data model framework.

As the reader progresses through this text, a framework for using a data model as part of their enterprise data architecture is described. Each chapter builds the readers understanding of the issues and techniques and in chapter 11 we summarise the fundamentals of the approach.

As a resident of the United Kingdom the non British readers might notice a few localisms that have crept into this text.

Examples of this include 'organisation' (not organization) and 'modelling' (not modeling). I can only offer my apologies for this but after years and years of writing this way I find it impossible to change. It's a case of the leopard can't change its spots.

I hope this text provides value to the reader and I would welcome any feedback.

Andy Graham

Director, Koios Associates Ltd

www.koios-associates.com

Forward to 2nd Edition

Over the last year I have had a nagging feeling that the enterprise data model story needed further refinement. This was partly because I felt the quality of the original wasn't good enough and partly because I felt the explanations given could be improved upon. In this forward I have therefore summarised some of the changes, so the reader can judge for themselves if it was worthy of upgrading from the first to the second edition.

Firstly, this edition has had more attention placed on the quality of grammar and spelling. This was an issue with the original which I can only put down to inexperience of the publishing process.

Secondly, I have had the assistance of the US military with this edition. Interestingly, soon after the original edition was released, I was contacted by a team from the United States Strategic Command (USSTRATCOM). Over time they have assisted me greatly by providing second opinions on some of the material, and I am confident that this version of the book is improved as a result. So many thanks go to David DeVol, Cathy Curry and Britt Anderson from USSTRATCOM.

I have added one new chapter and re-jigged a few of the existing chapters as follows:

Chapter 3 – added two new sections; the first on data as an intangible asset, the second on the business case for data quality.

Chapter 5 - added one new section on the role of the data architect. Also some of the content in this chapter has been moved to the new chapter 7 and some to chapter 8. This is to improve the flow and ease of understanding.

Chapter 7 – new chapter on business requirements and data processes.

Chapter 11 – added a new section on a maturity model for the enterprise data model.

Lastly, in addition to the new content a website with a number of free downloads has been setup. The details of this can be found in chapter 11, under 'closing points'

About the author

Andy Graham is an independent consultant specialising in data and information architecture As such he is primarily a hand's on person actively working with customers to develop their information and data management capabilities. Andy has worked over recent years with organisations across most industry sectors including financial services, government, utility, exploration, pharmaceutical, FMCG, telecom and leisure.

Andy was formerly Regional Manager of Sybase's Northern European Business Intelligence organisation. While at Sybase, he played a key role in building the BI organisation across EMEA and was instrumental in the delivery of many successful enterprise information solutions.

Prior to this Andy worked for Hummingbird (formally Andyne) as the UK Consultancy Manager, where he was responsible for the development of a full spectrum of professional services to complement the companies' software offerings.

Andy has also worked for Business Objects, where he was one of the founding members of the UK organisation and as such was responsible for the success of many customer implementations and information strategies.

Acknowledgements

I would like to thank my partner Angela for her support in this venture. Many an evening I've been locked away in the office working through this text until late into the night. We have been together for many years and her belief in me has helped more than she will ever know.

Over the years I've had the pleasure of working with many companies (too many to mention here) and I would like to thank them all. Each of them has contributed in some small way to this book.

Finally I would also like to thank the following individuals who have provided various nuggets of information that have been included in this book: Jamie Pinchen, Paul Highams, Joe Oates, Alex Slauson-Ross and Paul Perrin and as has been mentioned previously a special thank you to David DeVol, Cathy Curry and Britt Anderson from USSTRATCOM.

1. Introduction

"..... Only an initiate may understand ...."

Edgar Cayce, June 1932[1]

This book provides a framework for the enterprise data model, the business reasons behind it and the differences between conceptual, logical and physical data models. The question of how, and why, to use a data model artefact as part of the data governance toolkit for the whole enterprise is also addressed.

This publication is not an in-depth manual on how to model data for a new database system or your next design project. If that's the type of book you're looking for then please look elsewhere. It instead focuses at a level above these implementation projects and addresses the issues that organisations typically struggle with, such as:

- How do we provide a framework within which we can manage our data assets?
- How do we develop applications that adhere to a set of data standards; without creating a nightmare of administration and governance that is both unwieldy and unusable?

- How can we get business value from our enterprise data?

Although the concept of the data model has been around for decades, it is still not widely used beyond a purely physical representation of a database. There are many people out there that still believe the role of the data architect is just to create the database design for the next IT system.

It is the intention of the author to explain how the data model concept can be expanded into an enterprise framework for data. This framework can then be used as a key strategic weapon in successfully managing the enterprise's vast quantities of data. Along the way I also hope that the reader will gain valuable insight into some of the roles of the humble Data Architect.

Water, water, everywhere, nor any drop to drink

The line *'water, water everywhere, nor any drop to drink'* comes from the poem 'Rime of the Ancient Mariner', by the English poet Samuel Taylor Coleridge. The original poem was written in 1797-98, and first published in the Lyrical Ballads. The poem has influenced literature, films and music. For example 'Rime of The Ancient Mariner' is a famous heavy metal epic from the band Iron Maiden's 'Powerslave' album (released in the 1980's), a favour of the authors when a little younger.

The poem relates the events experienced by a mariner who has recently returned from a sea voyage. The tale depicts his nightmare journey to Antarctica after being thrown off course by bad weather. The ship and crew are then saved by an albatross that leads them out of the Antarctic.

The problems all start when the Mariner kills the albatross bringing bad luck down on the ship which is subsequently becalmed. The crew endures great hardship with all but the Mariner eventually dying. He is then stuck in the middle of the sea and because he is on the open ocean, the water is salty and unfit for consumption - thus his lament.

Day after day, day after day,

We stuck, nor breath nor motion;

As idle as a painted ship

Upon a painted ocean.

Water, water, everywhere,

And all the boards did shrink;

Water, water, everywhere,

Nor any drop to drink.

In 2008 the then UN Secretary General, Ban Ki Moon, remarked that water scarcity has the potential to fuel wars and conflict. This was based on some scary facts about water availability and consumption. Water constitutes about three quarters of the earth's surface, but only less than one percent of it can be used by its inhabitants; 97% is salt water and a further 2% is contained in glaciers.

This is not unlike the situation we find in today's data rich but information poor organisations. Companies are storing volumes of data so vast that we have invented new words to describe them; Kilo, Mega, Giga, Tera, Peta, Exa, Zetta and Yotta.

Introduction

Yotta, for those that don't know, is the largest named data number and represents 10^{24}. It was established in 2001 and is currently the largest number followed closely behind by zeta (10^{21}), exa (10^{18}) and peta (10^{15}).

In a recent article in the journal 'Science', it was calculated that the amount of data stored in the world by 2007 was 295 exabytes. The study showed that in 2000 75% of stored information was in an analogue format such as video cassettes, but that by 2007, 94% of it was digital.

Data, Data everywhere, nor any information to use

Only recently the data traffic on mobile phone networks exceeded voice call globally.

"Data traffic has exceeded the volume of voice calls across the world's wireless networks for the first time .....global data traffic nearly tripled in each of the past two years and forecast that it would double annually over the next five years..."

Extracts from the Financial Times on the 25th March 2010

Large data volumes bring with them usability, design and technology challenges. Although we have huge volumes of data only a small percentage is fully understood, of good quality and accessible. The humble data model is smack bang in the centre of this problem, as it provides one of the key weapons in an organisations data arsenal, and has the power to unlock the value that can be gained from these warehouses full of data.

The purpose of the data model

Probably the best place to start is with a clarification of the purpose of the data model. In a sentence we can define the data model as an artefact that allows us to explore data-oriented structures. It therefore follows that data modelling can be described as the act (or possibly the art) of exploring data-oriented structures.

To express this in more simplistic terms, a data model is a graphical method used to define and analyse data requirements. Associated to the diagram(s) are a series of data definitions. In essence the model describes what data will be stored and how it can be used.

Like other modelling artefacts data models can be used for a variety of purposes, from high-level conceptual data models to physical data designs. They can be used, for example, to define data in a standardised way for clarity of understanding. This allows development to be simpler and cheaper.

In essence it allows us to interpret, in diagrammatical form, the business meaning of data in a way that can be consumed by both business people and IT folk. Figure 1 below demonstrates this crossover between the business and the technology worlds.

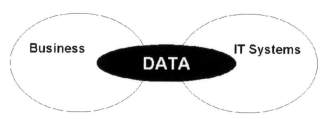

Figure 1.   *The relationship between the business and IT worlds*

I suspect this all sounds probably a little too academic. However it is not until you have actually used a data model, to discuss the data associated with a thorny business problem, that you really appreciate its value in crossing this divide. An example of this is when, a number of years ago, I worked with a major European insurance company and was trying to create a data structure to represent insurance risk. To make it even more complex, the challenge was to model risk across their general, life and health insurance business streams.

Initially there was a lot of scepticism especially because risk was considered an easy subject that didn't require any time with the business - IT could handle it. Secondly it was thought impossible to be able to build a model that worked across all three business streams. You can imagine the political hot house that ensued

The first meeting was with the general insurance team who started by telling me how risk was a simple problem to understand. "Everyone in the company understands it so why are we having this meeting" I was told. After some debate we sketched out a high level model showing risk as the central entity and the key entities it interacted with. I then asked the person to my left to expand on the entity 'risk' and provide me with a further level of detail. Within minutes of this conversation, the next person along was interrupting and before long the others in the room also jumped in with different views about different aspects. I then sat and watched the so called experts in risk spend the next thirty minutes arguing over how to define and decompose this single entity. At this point I must admit that I had earlier had similar discussions with the IT guy's so this argument wasn't a huge surprise at all.

What eventually became clear, after further workshops and meetings, was that it is possible to model risk data across all three business streams (life, general and health). The issues were more to do with real understanding of what the data actually means, political protectionism and vocabulary differences.

In essence it allows us to interpret, in diagrammatical form, the business meaning of data in a way that can be consumed by both business people and IT folk.

A bit of history

Prior to diving into the substance of this book, it is valuable to reflect on the roots of the data model. So where did data modelling start and why?

Back in the 70's, a 3-schema architecture was published by the 'American National Standards Institute' (ANSI) and its study group on database management systems 'Standards Planning and Requirements Committee' (SPARC). They recognised three levels in a database specification as shown in figure 2 below. The most important aspect of this new architecture was that it provided a separation of the physical storage structure from a logical representation.

Figure 2.   *ANSI/SPARC 3-schema architecture*

ANSI/SPARC	Relational Approximation
Conceptual schema	Base tables
Internal schema	Physical storage
External schema.	Views of data

Later in 1976, Peter Chen[2] published his famous paper on the Entity-Relationship Model. This paper provided a common specification language for three different types of database: relational, network, and entity-set. This was a step forward from the older 'Bachman diagrams'[3] in that it more closely reflected real-world terminology through the use of common symbols for relationships, whether one-to-many, many-to-many, binary or a higher degree. A year later, this common specification was being described by its author as a "pure representation of reality".

Chen's model was able to deliver a wealth of detail whilst retaining its elegant simplicity. These models were rapidly adopted outside the academic world, spawning generations of IT professional using these techniques.

Later James Martin's 'Information Engineering' streamlined Chen's work and removed some of the complexity around relationships. He modelled them as simple associates of binary form.

The need to support a three level database architecture (conceptual, internal and external) has now passed. The idea of a multi-layer process, beginning with a model (and modelling language) that more closely reflects real-world concepts, followed by a translation to an actual database schema, is still with us today.

Summary

As the importance of data grows it becomes imperative for organisations to find ways to understand and manage their enterprise data. This chapter has covered the background of the data model by discussing its history and purpose. We also started to explore why data is so important in today's organisations.

2. Information and Data

I know it may seem odd to have a chapter on information and data in a book aimed at data professionals (you would assume such professional would understand these terms). I have learned over the years never to assume anything. I believe it is important to clarify these terms as they often cause confusion and as the old saying goes 'it is better safe than sorry'.

Information and Data

Data is individual facts that have a specific meaning for a given time period. Data can be at the atomic level (for example 'date of birth') or derived (such as 'age'). Therefore if we take a person called John Smith who is born on the 1st September 1999 we have three pieces of Atomic Data (first name, surname and date of birth) and two pieces of Derived Data (full name and age). The full name is a combination of the first and surname whilst the age is derived from the date of birth.

Data can be considered as the basic building blocks used to create information as on its own it has no meaning. For data to become information, it must be interpreted and take on meaning. Information therefore can be defined as data that has been collected together to create some type of larger context than the individual pieces of data provide. In our example above we had data about a person. If we had a report or graph showing the average age ranges of employees within different types of roles and we were interested in such subject matter then we would have a set of information not data.

Data is individual facts that have a specific meaning for a given time period. Information is data that has context.

I will try and explain this using a different approach. Imagine we have the number 110110, it is not immediately clear what it means. It could be the date 11th January 2010 or 1st November 2010; depending on which side of the Atlantic you reside. It doesn't have to be a date what about a binary number which represents 54 or an actual amount of a transaction 110,110 with the currency unspecified.

If we assume for, the moment, that this number represents a banking transaction date of some kind. If we present this transaction date with a set of bank account details such as account number, type, description of the transaction, etcetera: the nature of this particular financial transaction becomes clearer. The last aspect of this example is actual information, whereas all the stages before were just pieces of data with varying degrees of definition.

DIKW

DIKW stands for 'Data, Information, Knowledge and Wisdom'. It represents the continuum from Data all the way to Wisdom. The diagram below shows the linkages between wisdom, knowledge, information and data.

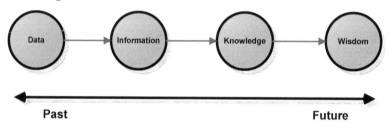

Figure 3.   *DIKW Continuum*

Knowledge is dramatically different to both data and information because it's highly subjective, personal and primarily found in people's heads. Each of us internalises knowledge based on perceptions, experiences and the information that is available to us. Knowledge management experts will talk about tacit and explicit knowledge. In the case of business intelligence and its impact on knowledge, we are referring primarily to explicit knowledge as it can be captured, acquired, created, stored and shared.

Explicit knowledge can be (or has been) codified, documented or explained. Tacit knowledge, on the other hand, is knowledge that is difficult to explain verbally, or in a document, or for that matter to store in a database. Maidenhead, for example, is a town in Berkshire (in the United Kingdom) and is a piece of explicit knowledge. The ability to speak English however is much harder to explain and can therefore be considered as tacit knowledge.

Wisdom can be defined as a deeper understanding of the knowledge gained, so as to be able to determine the optimum actions to take.

Enterprise Data

Enterprise data is data that has a value across the organisation. Not necessarily the whole organisation but has value outside one single database application and the department that owns it. Good examples of enterprise data are customer records. My customer details that I gave to the sales person in the mobile phone shop are valuable to many parts of the mobile phone company. The customer services team will pull up the records if I phone up with an issue or question. The billing department will use this data to calculate and post my bill. The marketing department will use my profile (some of which may be derived from my job type, age, sex, where I live, etc). In essence a large proportion of the departments within the mobile phone company will use the data from my customer records. Just think of the impact of the sales person in the shop not correctly taking down my details and the sales database not validating this data before sharing it with the rest of the organisation.

What is an enterprise data model?

It is also important to clarify what is meant by the term 'Enterprise Data Model'. In its simplistic form, an enterprise data model differs from an individual project based data model on two accounts – firstly it is at a higher level of abstraction and secondly it has a wider scope of coverage. It provides an integrated view of the data across the entire organisation. If we take as an example the definition of a customer data entity, we may have a collection of key attributes (name, address, etc) which are used by many different systems. Through an Enterprise Data Model we are able to provide a common standard in terms of definition.

The model takes the perspective of the whole organisation (or enterprise) and therefore the types of issues it addresses are at an enterprise level, for example the:

- Promotion of commonality, in terms of definition, across the various database applications.
- Reduction of risks associated with technology projects by providing organisational best practice for data.
- Improvement of the quality of data and associated business processes.

This list is not extensive, as the value of an enterprise data model is addressed in detail in the next chapter. The key point is that we would expect to see an enterprise data model only contain data that is of an enterprise nature i.e. 'enterprise data'.

An Enterprise Data Model promotes commonality, reduces risk and improves the quality of data.

A data model or information model (or any other variety of model for that matter) isn't a silver bullet for all known data related ill's. As an artefact (or series of artefacts) the enterprise data model should be used as part of a well thought out data architecture framework and strategy.

Summary

Information is valuable because it provides insight into problems and fuels business processes. Data is equally as important because it provides the atomic level elements that create information. This chapter defines the differences between information, data and enterprise data.

3. Pillars of Value

To compete in today's business world, you need information at your fingertips. It is often said that the industrial age was all about fossil fuels such as oil, gas and coal. It was these fuels that powered the world economies. Today, information is now providing the energy that drives the businesses of the economical advanced countries. Information is derived from data, which in turn in stored in the various database systems that underpin the business processes. This means we need well managed data to feed today's businesses, which in turn can be converted into information. As discussed in the previous chapter, information in its turn becomes knowledge and then wisdom which can then be acted on.

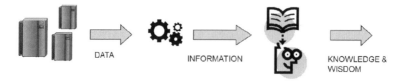

Figure 4.   *Data to Knowledge and Wisdom*

Data modelling is valuable to the enterprise because it provides a foundation upon which an organisation can achieve control, understanding and business impact via its data assets. This impact is achieved by improving the business processes and cutting the costs of both development and day to day operation.

The enterprise data model can be used, as part of a framework, to understand and manage this fragmented data and instil order and control.

Due to the increasing complexity of today's globalised marketplace (de-regulation, advances in technology and telecommunications, business consolidation and mobility of investor capital) problems with managing data have escalated. These trends have increased the complexity and speed of organisational change for today's businesses, resulting in a debilitating fragmentation of the data in the enterprise. The enterprise data model can be used, as part of a framework, to understand and manage this fragmented data and instil order and control.

Most businesses have strategies around sales, product development, investments, employment and property. This is because organisations recognise the importance of each of these subjects. Why not then have a strategy around the management of data?

Widget Ltd

In order to put this into an understandable business context, I will use an example. In time honoured tradition, let's imagine a manufacturing company called Widget Ltd. Widget Ltd is looking to streamline its manufacturing process by reducing the number of factories and therefore consolidating the manufacture of its product range. The business makes hundreds of varieties of widgets globally, driven by local market tastes and demands.

To drive the business transformation that Widget Ltd has embarked upon, the company needs to investigate the level of commonality of the widgets they are making to be able to understand the optimal number, configuration, and location of factories, warehouses and distribution centres. To do this the business needs to look into the numerous ERP systems that it has. The conclusion of this analysis is that each ERP systems stores data differently and that this data cannot be married up. This means that within each ERP system it is not possible, or at least highly complicated, to identify the commonality across the global supply chain of the different product attributes. This situation is typical of the state of play within many large organisations.

To understand the main issues, we need to look at some examples of the kind of problems that the company is facing. Figure 5 shows us an example product file from the European ERP system. It contains some basic product attributes such as Brand, Product Name, and Quantity in Pack.

The second example in Figure 6 shows a similar set of data structures but this time for the US ERP system.

Figure 5.   *European ERP system product file example*

Attribute	Definition
Brand	The name of the marketing brand.
Product Name	The name of the product as it appears on the pack.
Product Reference Number	The product SKU
Product Category	A high level grouping of products with similar capabilities.
Quantity in Pack	The number of products in a pack.

Figure 6.   *US ERP system product file example*

Attribute	Definition
Brand Family	A high level brand name.
Brand Name	A more refined brand name that is a subset of the brand family.
Product Name	The name of the product.
Product Code	The code used with the ERP system to uniquely identify the product.
Product Inner Quantity	The number of product within the inner packaging.
Product Outer Quantity	The number of product within the outer packaging.
Product Type	A high level grouping of product with similar capabilities.

It can quickly be seen that the file structures are not identical, however the impact of these differences may not be immediately apparent to the reader. To start with, the US brand data structure does not elegantly match with the European brand data structure. Also, quite clearly the European attribute Brand cannot easily be matched up with the US's two separate brand defining attributes 'Brand Family' and 'Brand Name'. If Brand is just a concatenation of Brand Family and Brand Name then this is not much of a problem. If on the other hand the attributes have different meaning, then a series of business rules will need to be defined and then implemented to link the brand data in the two systems together. This means that the marketing department may have difficulty in agreeing a common brand structure to use in marketing Widget Ltd's product ranges externally, whilst creating challenges in reporting and analysing results internally.

Figure 7.   *List of European Brand's*

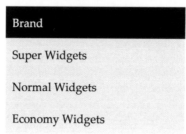

20

Figure 8.   *List of US Brand Family and Brand Name*

Brand Family	Brand Name
Hot Rod	Red
Hot Rod	Blue
Hot Rod	Silver
Special	Gold
Special	Black

As can be seen from the tables shown in Figure 7 and 8, and mentioned previously, the European and US data cannot easily be matched. Do we, for example, match The US Hot Rod Brand Family and Red Brand Name with Super Widgets, Normal Widgets or Economy Widgets. In reality we have to make an approximation based on a set of business rules or keep all the brand data from both the US and Europe separate. This results in no ability to compare, reducing the ability of the business to globalise the product range.

The sensible way forward is to rationalise the data definitions so that data can be treated in a common way. For example Widget Ltd could:

- Create a common brand attribute to group the like brands together, but without restricting the current flexibility built into the regional ERP systems.
- Conformity of definitions could be imposed so that both ERP systems would have the same brand

structure. Obviously this would require a large degree of internal negotiation.

Moving onto the next differences, we have the two Product Name attributes. Although on the surface they appear the same, they are not. The European Product Name represents the label version of the product name and the US Product Name is just a generic name which could end up being used for many different products, including those in Europe. Imagine trying to match 500,000 different products using their name (because each country uses different coding systems) when the names are not the same for equivalent products. Very time consuming.

One of the key foundations stones of MDM is an enterprise data model to govern the use and structure of the organisations data.

Some of the other issues that can be seen in the two product data files are:

- Product Reference Number and Product Code are not exactly the same piece of data; one is an internal system code whilst the other is a business reference number.
- Product Category and Product Type look to be the same, just labelled differently.
- Quantity in Pack matches with the Product Inner Quantity but then we are left with the Product Outer Quantity which has no equivalent in Europe.

Clearly it is complex to merge these two systems together, and therefore achieve the synergies outlined in the opening paragraphs of this chapter. Essentially, we need to make a series of decisions and compromises so that we can have the two systems synchronised into a single product definition.

This type of scenario is all too common and has been the instigation of many a data transformation project. The problem is caused by the implementation of multiple ERP systems from different vendors or from the same vendor just implemented differently. Even when they are all from the same vendor and the same version and on the surface have the same design, we find that the data standards they adhere to are not exactly standard.

Alternatively, we can look at a smaller scale example - a software company has two products; each with their own sales team and customer database due to a recent acquisition. Integrating the customer databases may cause problems such as different meaning of customer, different details held about customers or maybe even different ways of holding the address (one uses free hand text and the other is highly structured).

The Data Pillars

In the sections above we have discussed some examples of business issues that can be addressed if an organisations data is underpinned by an enterprise data framework. To allow us to explore further the business value proposition, we shall use a framework to structure our understanding which we shall call 'The Data Pillars'.

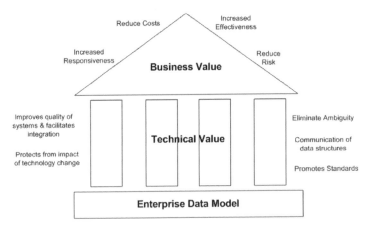

Figure 9.   *The Data Pillars*

The word 'pillars' is used because it encapsulates the concept that the enterprise data model is holding up the business. The diagram shown in figure 9 shows the three components of 'The Data Pillars' framework:

- Business Value; the business justification for our data related activity.
- Technical Value; the technical justification that supports the business case above.
- Enterprise Data Model; the enterprise level understanding of data.

Business Value

At the top we have business value. Data must add value to a business otherwise why spent time and money capturing, storing and managing it? The types of business value that can be realised can be summarised in the following points:

- **Cost reduction**; in our Widget example we are able to reduce the number of factories, warehouses, distribution centres, staff and a multitude of other costs. These reductions are only possible once we understand the product data characteristics from a global perspective and are able to streamline system and business processes.

- **Effectiveness of business initiatives**; it should be obvious to the reader that having a clear understanding leads to increased effectiveness of any business initiative. Imagine launching a company wide initiative to focus sales effort on the medium strength product range only to find the definition of medium differs in different geographies. In Africa, what we class as, medium strength could actually be low strength as the local tastes are different from Europe. If you think this is unlikely to happen, think again.

- **Reduced risk**; having clarity of understanding of Widget Ltd's product data allows the management team to make decisions based on facts; not assumptions, guesswork or even incorrect data. This in turn reduces risk, as decisions are based on a firm foundation.

- **Increased responsiveness**; with standards and commonality it becomes easier to introduce new products and use the existing manufacturing process and components. The levels of technical skills, experience and understanding are reduced.

Technical Value

Below the business value we have a series of technical pillars that hold up the business values. The pillars are: 'Eliminate Ambiguity', 'Communication of Data Structures', 'Promotes Standards', 'Improves Quality of Systems & Facilitate

Integration', and lastly 'Protects from Impact of Technology Change'. The following sections describe each of these pillars.

Eliminate Ambiguity

One reason that data and information modelling has become valuable to companies is that it provides a way of delivering a vast amount of meaning in an easy to consume way, whilst at the same time providing a high degree of clarity. The ambiguous nature of language means that a diagram can be used to express a concept that to do so via words would be a long and confusing document or conversation. Just think of the meetings you've attended where the minutes of the meeting don't reflect your understanding of events. Add to this the non phonetic nature of English (two words can share none, any or all of spelling, pronunciation and meaning) and then the global nature of business today and you have a communication nightmare.

'Ambiguous' - typically refers to an unclear choice between different definitions as may be found in a dictionary. A sentence may be ambiguous due to different ways of parsing the same sequence of words.

To push home these points and add a little humour into a relatively dry subject, I have included below a few headlines from real newspapers that can have numerous interpretations:

- Police Begin Campaign to Run Down Jaywalkers
- Safety Experts Say School Bus Passengers Should Be Belted
- Drunk Gets Nine Months in Violin Case
- Survivor of Siamese Twins Joins Parents
- Stud Tires Out
- Prostitutes Appeal to Pope
- Lung Cancer in Women Mushrooms
- Eye Drops off Shelf
- Enraged Cow Injures Farmer with Axe
- Miners Refuse to Work after Death
- Juvenile Court to Try Shooting Defendant
- Hospitals are Sued by 7 Foot Doctors

Just imagine having to explain these phrases to an audience whose first language is not English. Appendix A shows an example of how the headline 'Enraged Cow Injures Farmer with Axe' can be represented as a diagram to clarify its meaning.

Communication of data structures

A data model provides a way of communicating and identifying the basic data structure of the business, and its systems, without the need for specialised technical jargon. This means the business and IT can engage in discussions on changes and impact with equal involvement. By removing the technical noise (and therefore limiting the diagrams to key aspects of the data) we are able to discuss how data elements relate and interact with other data elements with business users of data.

It is common in IT projects to have to hunt around to find key information about an application that you are either working on or integrating with in some way. I would estimate that during a

6 month project with a small team of say 5, it would not be unreasonable to lose over a man month of time in re-doing analysis to clarify understanding of data that was done months (or years) before. In our Widget example you can imagine the design team having endless discussions with both the US and Europe to understand the differences between their ERP systems. An enterprise data model captures this shared understanding.

Promotes Standards

An enterprise data model facilitates the development and promotion of a standard, unified vocabulary for data. The introduction of standards is always a painful exercise, but if done correctly increases productivity and reduces costs. Within the Oil and Gas exploration industries, for example, huge amounts of money and time has been spent developing a series of data standards that provide a definition of key business data. This allows exploration companies and software vendors to exchange data and integrate software applications with greater ease.

Standards enable global (or just disparate) organisations to communicate between the different IT systems regardless of technology, purpose, design or vendor. This means that designers don't need to re-invent the wheel for each project.

Improves quality of systems & facilitates integration

An enterprise data model increases standardisation, improves clarity of definitions, and will over time improve the quality of IT systems. Quality can be represented in terms of quality of the actual software code, the 'fit for purpose' of the software or the quality of the data stored in the software application. This in turn reduces the complexity in integrating different systems together as they have a greater degree of commonality in data definition.

Another consideration is that a data model allows us to visualise the systems data structures before we actually build it. This is obviously desirable since design changes in general are 20 - 25 percent cheaper than code changes.

Increased standardisation and improved clarity of definitions will over time improve the quality of IT systems.

Protects from impact of technology change

During the life of a typical organisation, the various software applications that the business runs on are likely to change, be these upgrades or replacement systems. This creates dangerous opportunities for data definition divergences to sneak into the companies data.

Software applications that deal with the same subject matter don't necessarily all work in the same way, and therefore can have different interpretations of data and its associated definition. Imagine an inventory system with a product characteristic called 'Weight'. Due to historical reasons in the original system, it has been defined in pounds (lb). In the new replacement system which is based on the metric system the weight attribute is in Kilo's (kg). All the software applications that interface with the inventory system use either lb's for the weight characteristic or have adapters that allow them to speak to the inventory system. Therefore our one small definition change can have a massive cost implication as each of these systems will require some type of change and those changes could have knock on effects with other systems.

By making all software adhere to the companies' definitions of data, expressed via its enterprise data model, the business protects itself from the impact of changes in technology. In effect we are enabling the business to drive the use of technology not the technology drive the way the business works.

By making all software adhere to the enterprise data model, the business protects itself from the impact of changes in technology.

The Enterprise Data Model

Underpinning all of the above is our enterprise data model which is providing the enterprise level understanding and consistency of data. This is essential to allow an organisation to achieve these types of benefits. It can be thought of as the basis of any successful enterprise wide governance process for data. It's not sexy but is the foundation that all the business benefits outlined above are based on.

What happens if you don't have one?

Clearly, if you don't have in place a strategy for data architecture (specifically the enterprise data model) then all the benefits outlined above will not exist.

On an individual level this is not so much of a problem as someone who built a particular system is likely to know what data is what and where to find things. The problems start to occur once you have enterprise level systems that have multiple individuals working with them, that change over time and require to be integrated with other enterprise systems developed by other individuals.

Data definitions get confused, mutated and even lost. I remember issues such as this when working as a young BusinessObjects developer with a particular financial services client. The company was providing reports for senior management but it was unclear which definition from the three source applications that actually held the data was the correct version. The answer was never discovered and a work around had to be created.

There are many events in the course of a data elements life that can modify its meaning. If this is not managed all hell can, and probably will, occur.

Some thoughts on Data Quality

"Reports that say that something hasn't happened are always interesting to me, because as we know, there are known knowns; there are things we know we know. We also know there are known unknowns; that is to say we know there are some things we do not

know. But there are also unknown unknowns -- the ones we don't know we don't know."

US Defence Secretary (during the second Iraq war), Donald Rumsfeld.

A bit cheesy I know, but any text about data quality needs to refer back to this quote somehow. Since this famous speech was made in which Donald Rumsfeld basically says we don't know what we don't know this has become one of the traditional quotes to use when presenting on the subject of data quality.

Why is Data Quality an Issue?

We have all heard the stories of letters sent to dead customers either though the company has been told about their death or cheques sent out for £0.00. Companies are continuing to risk damaging their relationship with clients and their hard won professional reputation by paying too little attention to the quality and organisation of their customer data.

Data quality is an uphill struggle for most organisations because as volumes of data grow so does the proportion of dirty data. The popularity of software systems such as SCM (Supply chain management), ERP (Enterprise Resource Management) and CRM (Customer Relationship Management) has also highlighted these issues. Add into this mix the M&A activity over the last few decades and the cost cutting activities of the global recession and we have a problem.

A few years ago I experienced this myself with an incorrectly addressed letter from a well known office supplies business. Previously I had opened a new business account and six months later I received an introduction letter with a few money saving vouchers. The problem with the letter was that it containing an incorrect address (in fact the address didn't even exist as it contained two street lines in it), my name was spelt wrong, plus it containing vouchers that were three months out of date. Obviously I didn't deal with that company again. The point of this example is not to embarrass the company; hence they are not named, but to make the point that this is a common problem. The larger the organisation the more of a problem it becomes.

Given that it is a widely held view that the amount of data in organisations will expand a hundredfold over the next five years, companies must increasingly depend on and develop a coherent and cost-effective data quality strategy.

An enterprise data model improves data quality.

By data quality we mean more than just validating names and addresses or removing record duplication. It is a complete process for defining and enforcing global business rules for data quality.

The Business Case

The impact of data quality issues on an organisation can be difficult to express in a way that can be understood. It is obviously important to a business to make decisions based on correct information, but on the other hand once the costs involved are indicated companies can get cold feet.

To give an example of the business case behind these kinds of activities, let's look at a simplistic direct marketing example.

This example is used not because it covers all aspects of the issue (it doesn't) but because it can be easily understood. The marketing department has a customer database of 100,000 customers, and 2% of the addresses have a problem. There is a new product which the marketing department want to mail shot to this customer base. If we then assume a typical response ratio of something like 2%, and a cost per mail shot piece of £1 we get a breakdown as follows.

(A) Cost of each mail shot piece	£1
(B) The number of pieces mailed per marketing campaign.	100,000
(C) The cost of each marketing campaign. This is calculated as (A * B)	£100,000
(D) Typical conversion rate	2%
(E) Customers with incorrect addresses	2% = 2,000

Based on these numbers and a product that retails at £150 we get a comparison that shows a difference per marketing campaign of £6,000.

The breakdown is shown in the following table:

	With incorrect addresses	With addresses fixed
(F) Number of customers that are actually contacted (B – E)	98,000	100,000
(G) Number of customers that purchased the new product (F * D)	1,960	2,000
(H) Revenue from campaign (G * 150)	£294,000	£300,000
(I) Profit per campaign (H – C)	£194,000	£200,000

£6,000 is not a world shattering amount but if we then multiple this over a number of campaigns, and into the other areas of the organisation that use addresses, we can start to get a sensible figure for the impact of incorrect addresses. Combine this with the other data quality issues that probably exist in the data such as duplicate customers, incorrect customer profiles and we can get some sizable numbers.

A model can improve data quality

Data comes in rivers! By this I mean that data flows through an organisation like a river.

Upstream we have source applications which are normally transactional in nature. These systems are often the initial entry point for dirty data. By improving the effectiveness and consistency of data validation, we can then dramatically reduce our bad data.

Downstream we have Management Information systems, data warehouses and a wide variety of business intelligence technology. This data can pull together vast volumes of data, and rapidly deliver it to the data consumer.

Preventing data quality problems upstream, is generally considered easier and more cost effective that fixing it downstream. In the medical world they have a saying 'an ounce of prevention is worth a pound of cure'. In the IT world I believe the generally excepted rule of thumb is 1:10:100. One dollar (or pound) spent on prevention will save 10 dollars (or pounds) on correction and 100 dollar (or pounds) on failure costs. As one moves along the data river from data entry to data delivery the cost of dirty data escalates.

As I show later in this book, an enterprise data model is a sensible place to manage global data definitions including the business rules and validation rules associated with that data. An enterprise data model will improve the quality of data in the organisation by introducing commonality, shared definitions and governance processes. If data is managed as an enterprise asset the quality of a business' data will improve – over time.

Summary

Data is important to the welfare of an organisation. This chapter has outlined the arguments to support this viewpoint. Without well managed, high quality data organisations are running in an inefficient gear.

4. An overview of Data Modelling

This next chapter provides an overview of the techniques associated with creating a data model. It is not an extensive text as many good books have already been written on the subject, but should provide enough detail to serve as an introduction to the subject.

Data modelling has evolved as a diagrammatic technique to represent data entities and attributes and how they are related to other data entities and attributes. The method can be used with 3rd normal form data design or dimensional database design approaches as well as object based methods, although some of the diagram styles vary.

The essence of a data model lies in it's ability to efficiently represent complex structures, by removing uninteresting detail and replacing it with symbols. A data model drawn on a few scraps of paper can represent the data structures of a database which contains gigabytes or possible terabytes of data.

Notation

Data modelling uses a standard set of symbols to represent entities (groups of data) and the corresponding relationships between them. There are multiple sets of competing notation that can be used but within this text is shown one of the more commonly used notations (at least by the author).

The first symbol we need to know about is the entity. This data construct is something about which data will be stored. In this example the data group 'Product' can be identified as an entity. The entity is represented as a box with a title or name for the data grouping. Depending on the degree of detail of the data model our entity may have details such as attributes and keys indicated within the box.

Figure 10.   *An Example Entity*

The other key component of a data model is the relationship. A relationship is an association between two entities. The relationship is important as it mandates the conditions associated with the relationship that applies to all of the occurrences of those entities. The relationship is represented by a line that joins the two related entities.

Figure 11.   An Example Relationship

Entities

So what is an entity? The concept of an entity can be applied to almost anything that is significant to the business for example:

- Retail Businesses: Customer, Product, Transaction, Shop
- Financial Services: Customer, Account, Loan, Fund, Counterparty
- Exploration Companies: Well, Rig, Wellbore, Field, Survey
- Pharmaceutical: Pack, Ingredient, Drug Classification, Market

An entity type, also simply called entity (not exactly accurate terminology, but very common in practice), is similar conceptually to object-orientation's concept of a class – an entity type represents a collection of similar objects. An entity type could represent a collection of people, places, things, events, or concepts. Examples of entities in a banking system would include *Customer*, *Address*, *Transaction*, *Account*, and *Product*.

An entity is something about which data will be stored within the system under consideration.

A precise definition of 'entity' is not really possible, as they vary greatly in nature. In an exploration system, for example, whilst an oil rig is a physical object (entities often are) drilling is an event and an address is a location. However entities are nearly always those things about which data will be stored within the system under investigation.

Note that entities are always named in the singular; for example: customer, order and product, and not customers, orders and products.

Entity, Instances and Attributes

When we refer to an entity, what we are really discussing is a collection of instances of that concept. For example, an entity called car would have a number of instances which would represent different actual physical cars. It is the entity that is represented on any data model diagram not the individual instances.

Each entity has a number of more granular details defined for it such as the model of car, registration number, date of manufacture, colour etc. These detailed pieces of data are called attributes.

Relationships

Figure 12.   *Many-to-many relation between Product and Customer*

As mentioned earlier, a relationship is an association between two entities. This relationship is important as it mandates the conditions associated with the relationship. Figure 12 shows the relationship between a Product and a Customer.

Every relationship line shows two reciprocal relationships:

- that of the first entity with respect to the second
- and that of the second entity with respect to the first.

In this example a Product is purchased by a Customer and a Customer purchases a Product. A Product could be purchased by many Customers and a Customer can purchase many Products.

The relationship is the association between two entities to which all of the occurrences of those entities must conform.

Each relationship line has three properties: firstly the relationship phrase, secondly the cardinality of the relationship and thirdly the relationships optionality. These three properties combine to form the relationship statement.

Figure 13.   *Key to symbols used to show multiplicities*

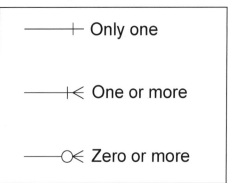

The list of multiplicities shown in Figure 13 is only a selection and is included as examples of modelling notation.

Data Modelling Approaches

There are a number of ways that data is structured; normalised, dimensional or object oriented for example. These approaches depend on the intended purpose of the data structure.

Normalise to Reduce Data Redundancy

Data normalisation is a process by which data attributes and data entities are organised to reduce the volume of data, whilst increasing the flexibility of the design. In other words, the goal of data normalisation is to reduce and even eliminate data redundancy.

Figure 14.   *Data Normalisation Rules.*

Level	Rule
First normal form (1NF)	An entity type is in 1NF when it contains no repeating groups of data.
Second normal form (2NF)	An entity type is in 2NF when it is in 1NF and when all of its non-key attributes are fully dependent on its primary key.
Third normal form (3NF)	An entity type is in 3NF when it is in 2NF and when all of its attributes are directly dependent on the primary key.

The concept of normalisation was defined by Edgar F. Codd, in the early 1970s. The table above summarises the first three rules of normalisation. Further detail and levels of normalisation beyond this table are outside the scope of this book.

De-normalise to Improve Performance

A normalised database can often suffer from performance problems. The reasons for this are fairly understandable. The normalised database structure has focused on reducing data redundancy, not performance, and therefore has data structures that required a large degree of query processing to get results from.

Within databases that need to be highly performant, we de-normalise the data structures. This means that we will have redundant data to aid performance. A typical approach is dimensional modelling of a database into a star (or snowflake schema). Further detail on these approaches can be found in the many books that are available on the subject(s) from authors such as Ralf Kimball etc.

Normalise to reduce data redundancy or de-normalise to improve performance.

Standards

Standards are one of life's painful necessities just like injections, diets and taxes. It's all too easy to disregard them as they can slow projects down in the short-term. The value in data standards is realised when one takes an enterprise approach. In the world of data standards examples would be:

- Naming standards
- Data attribute/entity definitions
- Data quality standards

Data attribute and entity naming standards, for example, should be used at both a logical and a physical modelling level. The logical naming conventions should be focused on human readability whereas the physical naming conventions will reflect technical considerations.

Standards aid understanding, improve quality and reduce risk.

Too often when you look at the definitions provided for an organisations data attributes, you find either blank or useless definitions. For example how many times have you seen definitions such as: the name of the product for Product Name or SKU for the attribute SKU and so on. It is important for standards to exist that stop quick, easy, but ultimately meaningless definitions being allowed into the data model.

Naming standards, for example, provides one weapon in achieving unambiguous understanding of an enterprises data. These types of standards provide consistency and clarity across the organisation, but only work if enforced.

Examples of such naming standard might be that all attributes must start with a primary term that provides some context to the data. Typically this would be the entity name. We might also enforce that that all data has a term to describe the type of data (eg date, amount etc). Based on these rules we could have:

- Employee birth date
- Employee salary amount

Employee is the primary term in both cases. Date and amount are used to describe the type of data in our example. This all means that for attribute two 'Employee Salary Amount' we know that the salary we are referring to here is the actual amount of the salary and relevant only to an employee.

I am going to gloss over the distinction between logical and physical data models at this stage, as the subject is covered in detail in chapter 6. Suffice to say that a logical model is a more business consumable version of the data model, and works at a higher level of abstraction than the physical data model.

Figure 15.   *Example data standards*

Logical Naming Standards	Physical Naming Standards
Each entity and attribute must have a full name that contains no abbreviations.	All table names should be prefixed with a single character and an underscore to indicate if the table is a real table, a view or a synonym.
All Entities and attributes must have definitions that are more than its name repeated.	Underscore must be used instead of spaces.

Data Model Patterns and Templates

Back in the 90's there was a major move from vendors such as Oracle, Sybase, NCR, IBM and others to sell into the marketplace data model templates. I remember this well on account of being part of the Sybase organisation doing exactly this with the IWS (Industry Warehouse Studio) range of templates.

The key idea behind these templates was the massive level of commonality between organisations. Based on this it is possible to develop a generic enterprise level data model template that will handle a high percentage of an organisation's data. For example most consumer focused companies will have data about the consumer such as name, age, sex, address etc., so why not make use of industry best practice in how to model this.

The table outlined in figure 16 gives some examples but only provides an overview of how these types of models can be structured.

Figure 16.   *Example data model template layers*

Template layer	Example Data Objects
Common Layer	Person; name, age, sex, address, etc
	Organisation; name, address, URL, directors, market sectors, number of employees, etc
Industry Specific Layer (Banking Industry)	Client: Bank account number, overdraft limit, account features, etc
Customisable Layer	Unique capabilities specific to the individual organisation.

The proposition behind these templates is based on a few key benefits:

- Risk Reduction because they are based on many man years of hands on industry expertise.
- Cost reduction through savings in deployment time.

Summary

This chapter has provided a brief overview of the art of data modelling. It introduces modelling notation, approaches, data standards and data model templates. The purpose of the chapter is to provide some foundations upon which to build the readers understanding.

5. Enterprise Data Architecture

"... logic clearly dictates that the needs of the many outweigh the needs of the few ..."

Star Trek II: The Wrath of Khan[4]

In the first few chapters of this book we explored some of the basic building blocks for our enterprise data model, such as the business justification, what is data and some data modelling fundamentals. We can now move on to the subject of how to use the data model within the context of an enterprise and more specifically enterprise data.

Typically, a data model is used for an individual project, with discrete timescales and objectives. With our enterprise scope we need to consider the wider organisational context of the data. We need to be able to manage the companies' data across multiple projects and over an indefinite timeframe. The Star Trek quote above captures this idea extremely well. In our context the needs of the whole organisation are more important and have larger consequences than individual projects.

Taking an enterprise perspective can seem intuitively wrong. Understanding data for the whole organisation, rather than just for your individual project, often goes against the grain. Project teams are typically delivery focused and this requires a mind-set that looks at only what is within the scope of an individual project; for a single application, department or function. With enterprise data we need to change our scope to be data bound rather than application, department or business function bound.

When a small team manage an individual database, it can seem like a nightmare of administration to consider the enterprise's needs. The individuals within the team know what data is in the database, what it means and how to use it. When we scale up and look at a number of databases across a larger organisation we find that not everyone is as familiar with every piece of data. Over time the meaning (and value) of the data changes. Data is modified and moved, definitions are amended, and in general data doesn't stand still. This means it is impossible for everyone to be sure of what data they are really using, every time they process a piece of data.

We must be focussed on our understanding of what data the business cares about, how it is used and what value is associated with it. It is too simplistic to assume that we need to manage ALL data within the enterprise. Although in an idealistic world this would be the scope, we need to be mindful of the real world we actually live in and take a far more pragmatic approach. To summarise we go back to Spock's quote *'the needs of the many'* is our primary consideration not *'the needs of the few'*.

Enterprise Architecture

Enterprise architecture provides an organisation with a framework in which to understanding the different pieces that comprise the enterprise. This includes such aspects as people, processes, information and how these components relate. Enterprise architecture allows the organisation to understand the enterprise components, and how they meet its current and future business strategy. Example frameworks are the:

- Open Group Architecture Framework (TOGAF), www.opengroup.org/togaf
- Zachman Framework, www.zachmaninternational.com

These frameworks typically divide the enterprise into a number of domains. The TOGAF framework for example, has three domains: 'Business', 'Information Systems' and 'Technology' architecture. Each of these is further divided into sub domains. The 'Information Systems Architecture' domain is subdivided into 'Information' and 'Applications'.

The Zachman Framework was developed in the 1980s at IBM by John Zachman. The framework provides a formal and highly structured way of viewing and defining an enterprise. It consists of a two dimensional classification matrix based on the intersection of six communication questions (What, Where, When, Why, Who and How) with six rows. The framework is not a methodology, rather it is a taxonomy for organising architectural artifacts. For example, it lacks specific methods and processes for collecting, managing, or using the information that it describes.

These frameworks all include aspects that look at the specification of information and/or data at various levels of abstraction. It would therefore seem appropriate that there is a close co-operation between the enterprise architecture team and the data architecture team.

Data Architecture

Where enterprise architecture provides an understanding of the components that comprise the enterprise, data architecture looks to understand its data structures. Data architecture describes how data is processed, stored, and used by (and between) systems. In this context a system could be an IT system or a people based process. It's the data that's important not the technology. Data architecture allows the organisation to understand enterprise data, and how this data meets its current and future business strategy.

The Role of the Data Architect

Often the data architect is seen as just a more senior and experienced data modeller. Yes, a data architect should be able to understand and develop data models, but there are many people on a company's development staff that will be able to do an adequate job at this as well.

The data architect is responsible for evaluating the use of data and relating data directly to the goals and practices of a company in a way that provides clear results. He or she must ensure the accuracy and accessibility of all important data, and is responsible for knowing what data is important and why. The data architect often acts as a middleman, deducing the data needs of a particular group and explaining the importance and use of the data most relevant to them.

The role of the Enterprise Data Architect is, in summary, to expand the company's use of data as a strategic enabler of corporate goals and objectives. To be able to fulfil this role, requires an individual who has a unique blend of technical, managerial and visionary abilities. Actual skills required, include all the obvious such as data modelling but also covers softer skills such as data governance, project management, business analysis and well as being quite a capable politian.

A Basic Data Architecture Framework

As data is fundamental to organisations, it therefore follows that the enterprise data model is a central element of any enterprise level data architecture. It allows us to understand and manage an organisations data, but it's not enough on its own. In addition to this central artefact, we need to develop a wider understanding of the enterprises data, covering subjects such as:

- Data Governance
- Data Mastery
- Business Requirements
- Data Flows and Processes

These additional areas allow us to flesh out our understanding of the organisations data beyond just a structural comprehension.

It is common in the IT world for a data model to be synonymous with data architecture. This understanding is incorrect; a data model doesn't on its own make a data architecture. What is needed is an expanded understanding of the data entities from the model into other aspects as bulleted above.

Figure 17 below shows a basic data architecture framework with its key components. Central to the data architecture framework is the enterprise data model. This component represents the backbone to the framework and hence is the central theme throughout this book.

Data architecture looks to understand the data structures of the business.

The diagram shows the various components that make up our data architecture framework with a brief explanation below. The subsequent chapters explore each aspect in greater detail.

Figure 17.   *A basic Enterprise Data Architecture framework*

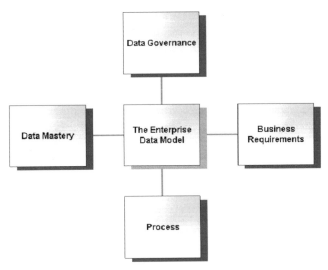

The Enterprise Data Model

The enterprise data model actually represents a series of models (not all focused on data), including Conceptual, Logical and occasionally Information models. These models work at differing levels of abstraction, just like layers of an onion. They reveal more detail as you peel away the layers.

Data Governance

Data governance can be thought off as an assurance process for the data that underpins the business.

Data Mastery

Where does the data originate from? Who owns it? How can we make sure we have the correct version of the customer record? All of these types of questions are addressed once we start to look at the mastery of our data.

Processes

Data is used by processes. Without data the processes would be meaningless. It is important, therefore, to have an understanding of the business process that use data and the technology processes that supply that data.

Business Requirements

Clearly we are not going to get far without some understanding of the business and the businesses requirements for data. In any initiative of this type, a significant investment of time is required from the business. Without their input this process becomes just another academic IT exercise.

Real Enterprise Data Architecture

Data is a complex beast. If you read any books (this one included) or articles on the subject, it all seems so simple. In the real world it's far from simple. Most of your companies' data will be held in legacy systems or packaged applications, both of these will have data structures where knowledge about these structures has been lost over the eons of time or held in locked vaults by the owning vendor. Other data will be held in spreadsheets and PC based databases which is in effect invisible to the IT department.

It is important to create powerful, simple, but effective models to understand the organisations data. The framework outlined in this and following chapters, introduces a series of techniques that can be used to complement the enterprise data model. You don't need to use all the techniques every time. The important thing is to develop an understanding of the enterprises data from an enterprise perspective to solve enterprise problems.

Most of your companies' data will be held in legacy systems ...

As the enterprise data model is the core focus of this book, the next few chapters explore that component of the framework in more detail. They provide an explanation of the different types of data models, and how they can be used together to support this approach. We also look at the other aspects of the framework which enrich this understanding of our data architecture.

Summary

This chapter introduces a basic data architecture framework, with the enterprise data model at its core. Supporting the enterprise model are a number of data architecture techniques that allow us to build a supporting data framework or context.

6. The Enterprise Data Model

In the previous chapter we touched on the enterprise data model, but didn't give a huge amount of clarity to what is really meant by the term. This chapter is intended to address this. It focuses on explaining what we mean when we refer to an enterprise data model; what are the key models that together make up this concept, and how do they interact?

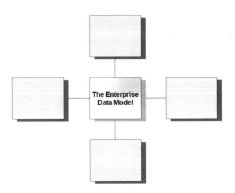

Overview

In use today you are likely to see three basic styles of data model (Conceptual, Logical and Physical) and occasionally two other types of models (Information and Canonical). These models work at differing levels of abstraction, just like layers of an onion they reveal more detail as you peel away each layer. The diagram below gives a high level view of the inter-relationships between these various types of models, within our framework. It uses the concept of three layers (Abstract, Logical and Physical) to group models together that work at similar levels of abstraction.

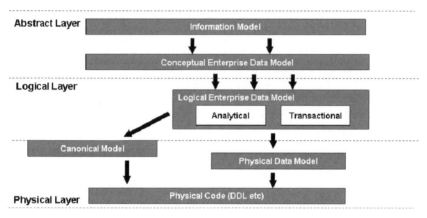

Figure 18.   Relationship of different model types

The top layer, called the abstract layer, contains the information model and the conceptual data model. They are at the same level of abstraction from the atomic level with the main difference being the focus of their intent. The information model is looking to understand and explore the information needs of the business whilst the conceptual data model as its name suggests is focused on the data perspective of the same business.

Next we have the logical layer which contains the logical data model. This model provides a fleshed out version of our conceptual data model, showing all data entities and their attributes. The model has a ying and yang aspect as it represents both the transactional and analytical sides to data.

58

Below this is the physical layer which contains our application specific models. The canonical model off to the left provides an interface focused version of our logical data model, that can be used to allow applications to integrate in a consistent manor. It is possible to argue either way as to the logical or physical nature of the canonical model. To me we are implementing the canonical model using XML which is basically a piece of code (all be it technology neutral) hence my interpretation that the canonical model is physical not logical. The physical data model provides the physical design required by the underlying technology and hence is technology specific.

This concept of model layers, which is expanded as we progress through this chapter, forms the fundamentals of our Enterprise Data Architecture Framework. It provides a way of abstracting away from the noise surrounding the data, and making our enterprise data model more consumable by senior managers and business folk.

Information Model

The term 'Information Model' is often associated with the internet as a technique for designing websites. In web design, the term describes the organisation of online content into categories and the creation of an interface for displaying those categories.

An information model is a technique for modelling the abstract business information needs and concepts.

The Enterprise Data Model

In chapter two we have defined information as data with context. The next question to answer is why does the enterprise DATA architecture framework include an information model?

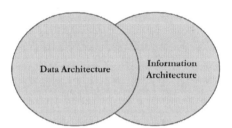

Figure 19.   *Data and Information Architecture Intersect*

In essence, data architecture is focused on the data needs of an organisation (data model design, data warehousing and MDM for example) whilst information architecture is focused on the information needs (for example knowledge management and business intelligence). The two are so heavily interlinked that I believe in order to do information architecture well you need an understanding of the data architecture.

Within enterprise data architecture, an information model is a technique for modelling the abstract business information needs and concepts of the organisation under consideration. For example within the world of old fashion branch banking we may have a number of key information elements such as:

- Customer Exception
- Loan Status
- Account Transaction
- Customer Value
- Customer Credit Risk

Reference Number	1.1
Name	Account Transaction
Definition	The information that relates to transactions that a customer or other party (including the bank) may perform on the customer's account.
Business Owner	Branch Customer Service
Also used by	Risk
Quality of Information	High

Figure 20.   *Information Element, Account Transaction*

An information model would look to capture the key details of these information elements, whilst at the same time understanding their interdependences to other information elements and there place in the overall business information landscape. Information elements are grouped together into information entities such as Customer, Product and Business Strategy. These entities are then plotted onto the organisation's business information landscape. This information map shows the relationship and importance of information to business functions and processes.

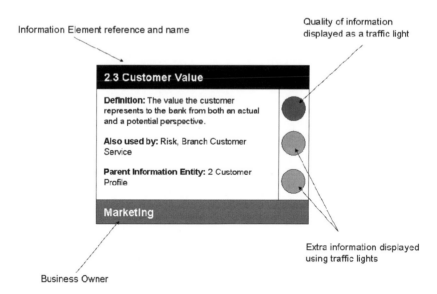

Figure 21.   *Information Element, Customer Value*

In figures 20 and 21 are shown some example information elements, Account Transaction and Customer Value, with some of the basic definitional details. Each information element has a:

- **Reference Number** – a number used to uniquely identify the information element. In these examples we have the reference numbers 1.1 and 2.3 which therefore imply we can have a group of information elements called an information entity. Maybe Account Transaction might be part of a higher level information entity called Customer whilst Customer Value may be part of a different entity called Customer Profile.
- **Name** – what we call the information element. The name should be immediately understandable by the

business as this model is business rather than IT focused.

- **Definition** - A textual explanation in business speak of the element.
- **Business Owner** – Indicates which part of the business has ultimate responsibility for this information.
- **Also used by** - Indicated the other business functions that use this information
- **Quality of Information** - a basic indication of the level of reliability of the information. This can be expanded to represent a wider data quality assessment.

If we further decompose each information element, we would find that each could be related to a number of business reports or processes. For example with 'Account Transaction', shown in figure 20, we could have inquiry reports, deposit/withdrawal reports, monthly statements etc.

Our first example shows a quite functional look and feel. It is normal with this type of model to create a more business consumable model as shown in figure 21. Clearly the look and feel would benefit with the introduction of colour, but alas this is not possible within this text as it has been printed in black and white.

How to create an Information Model

This section gives a very quick and dirty description of the process involved in developing an information model.

1. First, identify the different information entities used by the business.

2. Second, map these information entities to business owners.
3. Thirdly, identify who else uses this information
4. Lastly, iterate around this, refining the detail and definitions associated with each information entity and driving down the detail to arrive at information elements that underpin each entity.

Based on our Widget example from earlier we could end up with something like figure 22.

Figure 22.   *Information Matrix*

Information Entities	Marketing	Customer Service	Account Management
Customer Exceptions		Use	Own
Account Transaction		Own	Use
Loan Status		Use	Own
Customer Value	Own	Use	Use
Customer Credit Risk	Use	Use	Own

Conceptual Data Model

Conceptual data models (or domain models as they are sometimes named) are used to understand the high level data entities for the domain in question. This high-level model is equivalent to an architect's sketch plan. Its purpose is normally to support early exploration of options, including scope. Conceptual models are not like your normal data model as they don't contain much in the way of rigor. What we are after is the general feel for the key data entities and relationships. This model forms the framework we can use to undertake a more detailed analysis and design.

A conceptual data entity can be defined as a grouping of related data; for example customer, branch, product, transaction. An example is given in figure 23 below.

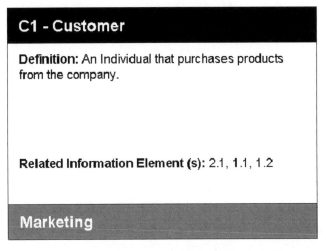

Figure 23.   *An example conceptual data entity definition*

Figure 24 shows a conceptual model for our branch bank based business mentioned in the previous section. The model provides an explanation at a very high level of how customer, branch, account, product, transaction and third party relate to each other. For example the conceptual data model shows that a customer can have one or more accounts with the bank. Each account is based at a single branch. Each account can also have a number of financial products (or features): these could be an overdraft facility, preferential interest rates, etc. The reader will note that the model itself is technically not correct as at this level it represents broad ideas not refined clarity.

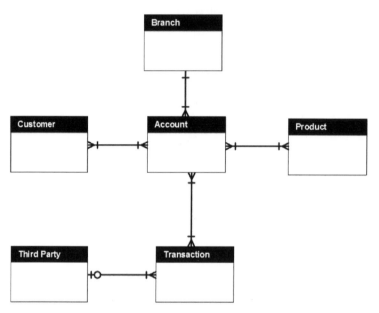

Figure 24.   *An example Conceptual Data Model for a bank*

Conceptual models are used to understand the high level data entities for the domain in question.

To give a sense of scale, a typical conceptual data model will have between 10 – 20 entities. I recently worked on a project that had over 350 physical tables in the physical data model whilst only having 17 conceptual data entities.

Subject Area Models

A Subject Area is an area of related concepts that are of interest to the enterprise such as investment, account, customer etc. Subject areas are not entities, instead they can be thought off as major areas of the organisation. They can have relationships, but if they do, these relationships represent general business linkages not E/R relationships.

Figure 25.   *Subject Area Model and Linkage to Conceptual Entities*

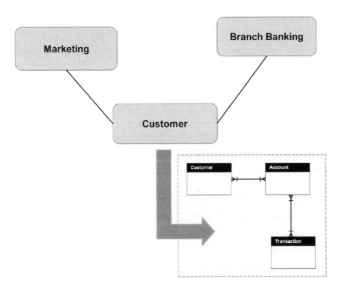

As shown above, in figure 25, we can use the subject area model and the information model to drive down to the next level of detail by identifying key conceptual data entities contained within them.

Logical Data Models

Logical data models are used to understand a business domain in greater detail than a conceptual data model can. At this level we are looking at a model that has a high degree of similarity, at least on first glance, with a physical data model but is actually technology neutral in design and has a level of abstraction from a harden physical design.

A logical data model is a decomposition of the conceptual data model.

Typical uses of a logical data model are to understand the data used in a single project, single business function or for the whole organisation. They depict the logical entity, the data attributes describing those entities, and the relationships between the entities. Each entity would have attribute details included. These attribute details would be repeated for each attribute within the logical entity.

Figure 26.   *An example of a logical entity definition*

Entity Name	Customer
Entity Definition:	An individual that purchases products from the company.
Business Owner of Entity	Marketing
Parent Conceptual Data Entity	Customer

Attribute Name	Product Reference Number
Attribute Definition	The unique reference number for a product.
Data Type	Alphanumeric (20)
Master Data Source	Product Marketing database

Figure 27.   *An example of a logical attribute definition*

Figure 28 represents a logical data model of the customer entity from our conceptual data model shown in figure 24. It shows the logical structure that the data has with the attributes and relationship information (ooops forgot the relationship names). We can see from this model that a customer can have multiple addresses and these are managed through an intersection entity that handles the purpose aspect of each address. This means that as a customer, I might have a correspondence address and a residential address.

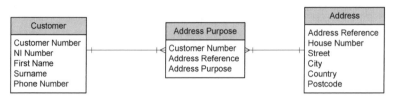

Figure 28.   *A simple logical data model for a customer conceptual entity*

Analytical and Transactional

As the logical model is used to drive the design of physical systems it needs to be able to support both transactional (OLTP) systems and more analytical (OLAP, Data Warehouse/Data Mart's etc). From an enterprise perspective we will need to develop both types of model. This means in practice that a logical model can be analytical based (star or snowflake) or more transactional (3rd normal form).

We would also expect to have enterprise level mapping from the transactional logical model to the analytical logical model as shown in the diagram above.

Figure 29. *Normalised to Dimensional mapping*

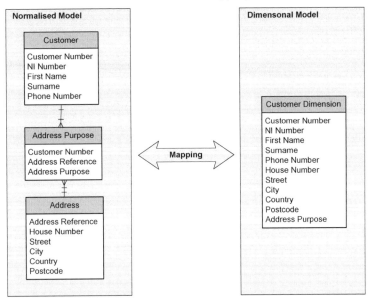

Conformed Dimensions

A dimensional structure is the typical way that analytical based data is modelled. When we refer to an enterprise dimensional model, as in the section above, we are really referring to a library of conformed dimensions. This means in practice that a series of conformed dimensional structures would typically be created to support the organisations enterprise analytical needs. The word conformed is important as it means that the organisation would typically use the same (or a subset off) structures across the organisation whenever there is an appropriate requirement.

For example, we may define an enterprise level dimension for a customer which will map directly onto the transactional logical data model. This means that for any given attribute in our dimension, we will know the corresponding attribute in the transactional logical data model.

Physical Data Models

Physical data models are used to design the actual schema of a database, depicting the data tables, the data columns of those tables, and the relationships between the tables.

Although logical and physical data models sound very similar, the level of detail that they model can be significantly different. This is because the goals for each model are different – you can use a logical data model to explore domain concepts with your stakeholders, and the physical data model to define your database design based on the technical constraints of the technology platform.

Physical data models are used to design the actual schema of a database, depicting the data tables, the data columns of those tables, and the relationships between the tables.

Figure 30 shows the physical data model derived from figure 28. Notice how the physical data model shows greater technical detail from the logical version. Physical data models should also reflect your organisation's database naming standards, in this case an abbreviation of the entity name is appended to each column name, an abbreviation for "Number" was consistently introduced and a single letter is appended to each entity name to let you know if it is a table or a view.

Figure 30.   *An example physical data model*

Physical vs. Logical

To illustrate the differences between the logical and physical data models a few examples are probably necessary.

Entities and Tables

Logical data models are comprised of data entities whilst physical data models are comprised of tables. Many people use these words interchangeable (I've done this many times myself). In reality they are very different. An entity represents a set of cars, planes, oil rigs or other concepts that are important to the business. A table is an actual data structure implemented within a particular database technology that contains data and is physically stored on a disk. The difference is the technology specific nature. We may have a logical entity called 'Customer' that depending on the technology maybe:

- Physically implemented as an actual table

- Defined as a set of meta data within a metadata driven technology.

- Implemented as a view on top of some of a person table.

Many-to-Many Relationships

Typically in a 3rd normal form data model, we explode out many-to-many relationships into two separate relationships and an intersection entity. I have always considered this to be a purely physical concept as what is really occurring is that we are defining the actual implementation of the many-to-many relationship. The intersection table is just part of that relationship definition and holds no business data. Therefore, in a logical model we would expect to see many-to-many relationships whilst in the physical model we would expect them to have been resolved via an intersection table.

You may have noticed in figure 28 and figure 30 that we have what on first glance looks like an intersection entity. Address Purpose actually contains a piece of business data (in this case the purpose of the address) and hence is a valid logical entity.

Canonical Models

A canonical data model is an application independent model that allows application to produce and consume messages in a common format. The canonical data model specifies all the XML constructs for inter-application messages.

In any given communication, there will always be a transformation from the local format on the sending side to the canonical format. And conversely there will always be a transformation from the canonical format to the local format at the receiving side. These rules apply even when the local format is identical to the canonical format. This null-transformation makes the whole process generic.

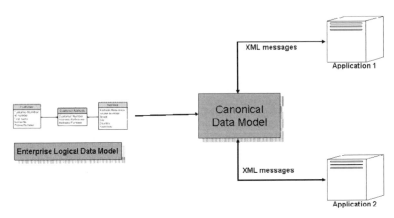

Figure 31.   *Overview of a canonical data model architecture*

To understand an example is needed. Imagine we had a master definition for customer data that we wished to use to improve integration between our customer database and our accounts system. We would define the canonical schema for customer derived from our enterprise logical model definition for customer. Then we would the implement our canonical schema definition as a series of XML (and/or XSD's) within each application. This provides us with a way of managing and validating the data involved in the integration.

The canonical model is in reality a physical model typically defined using XML, although this is not mandatory. It is used not as a database but as an integration model for data. The canonical schema is derived from the companies' enterprise logical data model just like a physical data model would.

The Enterprise Viewpoint

The above models form the backbone to the data architecture framework. We have three model layers with different purposes and roles. The table below shows for each model layer its purpose and the key consumers of these artefacts.

Figure 32.   *Different Model Types*

	Abstract Layer	Logical Layer	Physical Layer
Model Types	*Information Model, Conceptual Data Model, Subject Area Model*	*Logical Data Model (analytical and transactional) and mappings between both.*	*Canonical Model and Physical Data Model*
Purpose	*To understand the high level needs of the enterprise.*	*Detailed understanding of the data needs of the business.*	*Represents the physical design.*
Key Consumers	*Business and senior IT folk.*	*Business and IT*	*Primarily IT*

What is the Enterprise Data Model

So what is the Enterprise Model? It is the first two layers of our series of models. It comprises the information model and the conceptual data model from the abstract layer. Also, it is made up of the logical data model(s) from our logical layer.

This three level concept is similar to an onion; in that it is made up of layers. The layers allow us to manage the amount of detail that is presented within each level via a series of artefacts design for particular audiences and purposes.

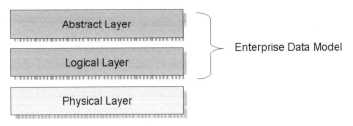

Figure 33.   *The enterprise data model*

It is impossible with the human brain to capture all of this detail: hence we split the detail within layers of gradually greater and greater depth. Using this framework we can capture the vast complexity of the enterprise via a series of interlinked artefacts.

Summary

Within this chapter we have looked at a way of decomposing the different types of information and data required to understand an enterprises data needs. Our framework has three layers: the top layer, called the abstract layer, which contains the information model plus the conceptual data model. Next we have the logical layer which contains the logical data model. Below this is the physical layer which contains our application specific models. This concept of model layers forms the fundamentals of our 'Enterprise Data Architecture Framework'.

7. Needs and Process

Introduction

Clearly we are not going to get far without some understanding of the business and its data needs. Supporting this are processes that manage the data or underpin the business usage of it. This chapter looks at how some understanding of these areas can be incorporated into the EDM.

Business Needs

In this context we are really meaning the business requirements for data, information and the processes that this data and information require. This may come in the form of report specifications or through a more detailed analysis of the corporate

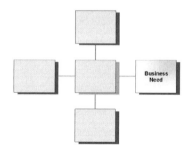

data and information needs.

When looking at business needs we have a number of ways that we can express this, namely:

- Business Case
- Business Value
- Business Usage

Business Case

We have already looked at the business case aspects in the chapter on the pillars of value. It is important that this is not overlooked. A viable business case should be developed and should grow with the enterprise data model.

In chapter 3 we looked at an example centred on a company called Widget Ltd that was experiencing product data definition issues. We could quickly see that having one enterprise view of product data would have great benefit to Widget Ltd. It would reduce costs and increase business efficiency, by simplifying the infrastructure required to manufacture and distribute widgets globally. Based on this it should not be too difficult to build a financially viable business case to support the work.

Typically, we would expect to have a fully documented and approved business case for the whole EDM strategy. It is expected that this business case will evolve and develop with the EDM and not become a static reference document.

Within the information model it is possible to build business cases that support various elements within that model. In chapter 6 we used the information element 'Customer Value' as an example. We might find that this information has a business case backing it, due to various initiatives and projects in this area.

Business Value

Over the last few decades commerce has changed from being biased towards tangible assets (such as factories, stock, property and physical products) to more intangible assets (such as intellectual property, marketing brands, IT systems and the data that resides in them). Research from the US has shown that the average market-to-book ratio of companies in the S&P 500 rose from just over one in the early 1980's, 3.5 in the mid 1990's to 6 by 2000, falling back to 4.5 by late 2003. A market-to-book ratio of 4.5 implies that the tangible assets of a business account for less than 25% of the value that investors are placing on a company. In essence intangible assets have supplanted tangible assets as the key value drivers in today's economy.

N.B The market-to-book ratio is used to find the value of a company by taking the book value (calculated by looking at the firm's accounting value) and dividing it by its market value (determined by its stock market capitalisation)

During the same period traditional accounting has remained tied to tangible assets. This means that a significant percentage of an organisation's assets are under reported in the company's accounts. It is a generally agreed management view, that you cannot manage what you cannot measure. Therefore many of the assets that are most responsible for creating organisational value are not managed very well.

The classification of intangible assets is in its infancy. Based on the current research in this area four areas of intangible assets can be identified:

- Knowledge: intellectual property (patents, recipes, product research), industry experience and knowledge (such as manufacturing and operating guides and manuals), IT systems and the data that resides in them.

- Business processes: innovative business models, manufacturing techniques and supply chain operations.
- Market Positioning: contracts, distribution rights, licences (eg third generation telecom licences), import quotas, government permits etc.
- Brand and Relationship: trade names, trademarks and trade symbols, domain names, design rights, trade dress, packaging, copyrights and the brand relationship with the consumer.

Some examples of real world companies that have business models based on (or heavily impacted by) intangible assets

- Google purchased Motorola Mobility Holdings for over $12 billion to forestall patent litigation and force settlements with Apple Inc. (AAPL) and Microsoft Corp. (MSFT) over smartphone technology.
- ARM Holdings, a circa $1 billion company, is the world's leading semiconductor intellectual property (IP) supplier.
- Dun & Bradstreet is the one of the world's leading source of business information and insight for credit risk management, sales & marketing, supply management and regulatory compliance decisions worldwide. They have a huge commercial database containing more than 202 million business records.

The purpose of valuing the organisation's enterprise data is not about getting the exact value (if this is at all measurable) but to give a sense of the importance of this type of data to the organisation. It is easier to manage and understand things that can be valued rather than nebulous data concepts.

Calculating the value of your data is in its infancy. If the reader wishes to know more I would suggest 'Intangibles' by Baruch Lev[5]

Business Usage

To understand how the business uses (or could use) the enterprise data we need to look at the data from many angles, namely:

- Information Architecture: We showed in chapter 6 that it is possible to model the information needs of an organisation. Information can be captured at a high level such as 'Customer Value' or a more granular level such as a report of the top ten customers within each sales region. These can be mapped to the associated data entity/attribute depending on level or granularity of models and levels of sophistication you wish to capture this at.
- Business Requirements: If they are documented at an appropriate level it should be possible to link some business requirements to particular pieces of data.
- Application to Data Matrix: Understanding the applications that use different data entities via a application to data matrix can provide an alternative but easier way to understand usage of data. This matrix allows the organisation to determine what data is used by which application.

Processes

Data is used by processes. Without data the processes would be

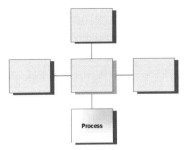

meaningless. It is important therefore to have an understanding of the business processes that use data, and the technology processes that supply that data. There are many techniques for modelling and understanding processes; two examples, DFD and CRUD, are included below.

Data Flow Diagrams

Data flow diagrams (DFD) allow us to understand how data is processed by systems within the enterprise in terms of inputs and outputs. It achieves this via a graphical representation of the flow of data through the various IT systems within the organisation under consideration.

We are interested in understanding the movement of data because it's essential to organisations to have the right information, in the right hands, at the right time, to make the right decision. As we have discussed earlier, information is derived from data hence the need to understand the flow of data.

We understand this movement by creating data flow diagrams. These diagrams allow us to understand how the key data moves within the organisation, from one application to another.

The Process

The first piece of notation to mention is the process, which is represents as a circle. The process transforms inputs into outputs. To be more specific it represents the part of the system that changes inputs into an output

The Flow

We next have the 'flow' which is represented graphically by an arrow with a name annotated next to the arrow. A flow shows us the movement of data between parts of the system. It is worth being aware that for most DFDs the flow represents data but they can also be used to model systems other than data; for example physical material.

2. Orders

The Store

Data at rest is called a 'store' and is represented by two parallel lines. It should be noted that a store although often a database doesn't have to be; it can be microfiche, a spreadsheet or a paper based filing system

1. Customers

The Terminator

17. Supplier

The next component to look at is the terminator. The terminator is graphically represented as a rectangle. It represents entities that are external to the system (ie the outside world). These entities are shown as they are involved in communication with the system being represented. Typically, a terminator is a person or a group of people.

The numbers shown above, for each figure, represent an identification reference which can be used in any supporting documentation that explains the item in more detail.

An Example

How does this relate to our enterprise data model? At each level of the model we can include DFDs (see below) showing the flows and data stores that each data entity (conceptual or logical) relates to.

Figure 34.   *Data Flow and Linkage to EDM*

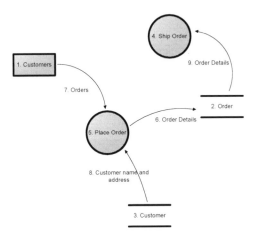

Using this example we would get something like the following:

Conceptual Data Entity	Data Stores	Flows	Process
Customer	3. Customer 2. Order	7. Orders, 8. Customer name and address, 6. Order Details 9. Order Details	5. Place Order 4. Ship Order
Product	2. Order	7. Orders 6. Order Details 9. Order Details	5. Place Order 4. Ship Order

Order	2. Order	7. Orders	5. Place Order
		6. Order Details	4. Ship Order
		9. Order Details	

CRUD

One tried and tested technique to map data onto business processes is via the use of a CRUD matrix. A CRUD matrix should be developed for each key data element.

The CRUD matrix is a table showing the functions that affect our enterprise data which are **C**reate, **R**ead, **U**pdate and **D**elete - hence the name. The purpose of this matrix is to illustrate the relationships between business processes and the data they use. At certain junctures where a process column meets a data class row, there will be the letter C, R, U, or D. Certain process will create data and others may read the data, while still other processes could update that data.

Figure 35.　　*Example CRUD Matrix*

	Customer	Order	Account	Stock
Create Order	C	U	R	R
Modify/Maintain Order	U	U		
Process Order	R	RU	RU	
Invoice Customer	R	R	CU	R
Shipping	R	R		CU

Typically you would create a CRUD matrix for each user group or for each data entity. My preference is to drive this from the entities in our higher level conceptual data model. This means we end up with a CRUD matrix for each conceptual data entity. The example above shows a CRUD for four key data entities: Customer, Order, Account and Stock.

Other options are to map applications to processes via a matrix. This matrix can then be used to help identify which applications support the different business areas.

Summary

This chapter has addressed how we weave into our data framework process and business requirements. We have looked at a few standard ways of addressing this. It is important to remember that adding details about processes and requirements should be handled with a highly pragmatic hat on. The intention is to widen the organisation's understanding of the value and purpose of its data. It would be impossible to do this overnight. Instead this should be seen as a slow burn activity that will grow in richness over time. As it grows, we will have a better understanding of the impact of changes to data and identify opportunities for efficiency improvements through the elimination of data redundancies.

8. Master Your Data

A book on enterprise data modelling wouldn't be complete without at least a reference to the ideas of Master Data Management. In our framework, data mastery represents this area. The intention of this chapter is to provide an overview of Master Data Management or MDM, as it is typically called, and how it relates to our enterprise data model.

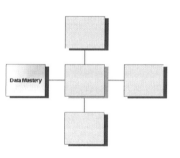

What is MDM

The objective of MDM is to provide and maintain a consistent view of an organisations core business data; this may involve data that is scattered across a range of applications. Typical examples include Customer, Product, and Supplier. It is in reality the reincarnation of the problem of how to manage the consistency and integrity of the myriads of data assets that exist across the enterprise. Systems such as ERP, SCM, CRM, BPM, ODS, data warehouses/marts, legacy applications, ECM (unstructured content like emails, documents, etc), portals and various home-grown applications. Each of these applications generates and works on a data set which partially or completely overlaps with the others. The same Customer, Product etc is often represented in two or more applications, sometimes differently. The objective of MDM can be therefore summarised as providing a consistent view of an organisations dispersed data and its associated definitions.

It is a natural evolution that the enterprise data model has become a bedrock of companies MDM strategies. To implement a MDM strategy successfully, a company needs to understand all its enterprise level data as master data is enterprise by definition.

The enterprise data model is the foundation that MDM is built upon.

Master data is often one of the key assets of a company. It's not unusual for a company to be acquired primarily for access to its customer master data. There are also a number of companies that have created highly lucrative business models based on selling data about specific marketplaces (examples include Reuters, Bloomberg, IMS Health and Dun & Bradstreet).

The Silk Road Story

To explain the MDM challenge in non IT terms I have included below the story of 'The Silk Road' as it provides an approximation of the issue but set within a historical context.

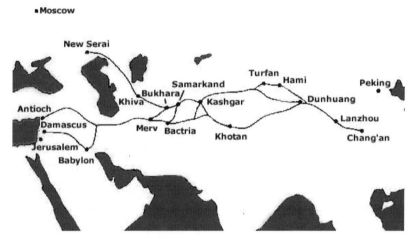

Figure 36.   *The Silk Road[6]*

The Silk Road is an extensive interconnected network of trade routes across the Asian continent that connects Asia with the Mediterranean and Africa. The description of this route as the `Silk Road' is somewhat misleading. Firstly, although the word road implies a continuous journey, very few travellers traversed the route from end to end. Typically, goods passed through a series of agents. Secondly, no single route was taken; crossing Central Asia several different branches developed. Extending for over 4,000 miles this route was not only a conduit for silk, but also for many other products.

The route was extremely treacherous. The Chinese monk, Faxian, gives us an inkling from the accounts of his travels along the road at the end of the fourth century:

"The only road-signs are the skeletons of the dead. Wherever they lie, there lies the road to India."

Faxian, 399 to 414 BC[7]

As has been mentioned silk wasn't the only precious commodity traded. Caravans heading towards China carried gold and other precious metals, ivory, precious stones, and glass, which were not manufactured in China at that time. In the opposite direction furs, ceramics, jade, bronze objects, lacquer and iron were traded. Many of these goods were bartered for others along the way, and objects often changed hands many times. There are no records of Roman traders being seen in China[8], nor Chinese merchants in Rome. In essence silk passed from China to Rome passing through many agents meaning that:

- The Chinese never knew where the silk went
- The Romans never knew where it came from

This is the crux of the MDM problem:

- The Data Producers never know who is using their data
- The Data Consumers never know where their data comes from
- The skeletons of the dead mentioned in the quote from Faxian can relate, in our context, to failed projects that didn't consider the enterprise nature of data.

People, Process and Technology

It is common for MDM to be considered as a technology but, as the diagram below shows, in reality it is a combination of people, process and technology.

- People represents the data owners, data stewards and executive sponsorship that allows this to occur.
- Process represents the governance mechanism and standards guidelines. These governance processes

assist the business (and IT) in their day to day
interactions with the organisations data.

• Technology represents the IT systems that provide
support to the people and process elements above.

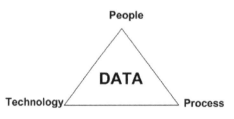

Figure 37.   *MDM components*

Many companies assume when they embark upon a MDM
initiative that all they need to do is buy the latest and greatest
MDM software and all will be wonderful. Alas this whole sector
is made up of a myriad of vendors solving many different
aspects of the MDM challenge. I have personally encountered
many companies that have defined their MDM strategy based
on a proposal/presentation from a software vendor. Companies
need to understand and define their own interpretation of MDM
and supporting processes prior to buying anything. If they don't
understand their companies' real MDM requirements, they risk
solving the wrong problem or worst creating new ones.

The truth about data

In chapter 2 we defined the differences between information
and data. We defined data as:

Data is individual facts that have a specific meaning for a given time period.

And information was defined as:

Information is data that has context.

We didn't really take that definition much further, except to distinguish between atomic and derived data. In this section we will subdivide our data definition further.

There are essentially six types of data that a company stores within its corporate databases:

- Metadata
- Reference Data
- Transaction Structure Data
- Enterprise Structure Data
- Transaction Activity Data
- Transaction Audit Data

This section provides some definitions for each data type. The reader is encouraged to re-read chapter 2 prior to continuing.

Metadata

This is often referred to as data about data; this means it is data that describes other types of data such as the structure of a database.

It is often found in a database's system catalogue and sometimes included in database table definitions. Metadata is not directly used to run or manage the enterprise. It is often used by IT staff to assist them in their work, or business users to help them use IT resources.

One often overlooked aspect of metadata is that it's not just "data about data". It can, for example, include descriptions of networks or may represent a set of business rules used by an application. An example of metadata would be the definition of a data element such as Product Reference Number or Customer Status.

Reference Data

Reference Data is any kind of data that is used to categorise other data found in a database. Alternatively it can be used to relate data in a database to information beyond the boundaries of the organisation. This type of data is also known as: Lookup Data, Domain Values or Codes and Descriptions. Tables containing reference data usually have just a few rows and columns.

ISO 3166-1-alpha-2 code	Country name
AF	AFGHANISTAN
AX	ÅLAND ISLANDS
AL	ALBANIA
DZ	ALGERIA
AS	AMERICAN SAMOA
AD	ANDORRA
AO	ANGOLA

Figure 38.   *ISO 316 country code and short name standards*

A good example of reference data are country codes and names as shown above. This list is an excerpt from a list published from the ISO standards bodies' website.

A company may tag a transaction record with the country that the transaction occurred within. The actual definition and values for a country are defined outside the company. In figure 38 our example shows a sample of the ISO codes and names for countries. This list is sourced from the ISO standards body which in turn is sourced from the United Nations.

Transaction Structure Data/Core Business Data

Data that represents the direct participants in a transaction, and which must be present before a transaction can be fully understood e.g. Customer, Product and Supplier. This data is often considered as the businesses core business data. Transactions typically need to be related to this type of data so as to give the transaction some meaning and purpose.

Without transaction structure data there would be severe consequences for the organisation in question. Imagine what would happen to a bank if it lost or had corrupted some (or all) of its customer data. Or the consequences of not knowing which deposits related to which bank account.

Enterprise Structure Data

Enterprise structure data is data that describes the important structures that exist within the organisation, more commonly referred to as 'hierarchies'. This data permits business activity to be reported or analysed by business functions or by product grouping.

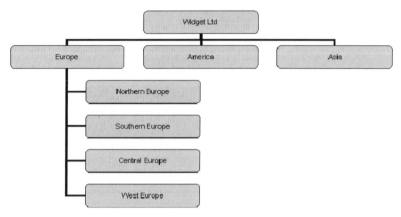

Figure 39.   *Widget Ltd organisation structure*

Using our Widget example from earlier, we could have an organisational structure as shown in Figure 39 above. Within our enterprise structure data we would have enough data to be able to explain the hierarchy to any consuming system.

Transaction Activity Data

Transaction activity data is data that represents the operations (actual business transactions) that the company carries out; such as dates and amounts. Examples would be:

- Dates of invoices and the amounts for each line item
- Dates of customer meetings and events
- Dates that geological measurements are taken

Transaction Audit Data

Data that tracks the life cycle of individual transactions such as audit trails and server logs.

So what is Master Data

So back to the question of what exactly is master data. We earlier defined master data as enterprise data. If we apply our definition of enterprise data (which is data that is important to the enterprise rather than any single project or business function), we should then be able to re-define what we mean by master data.

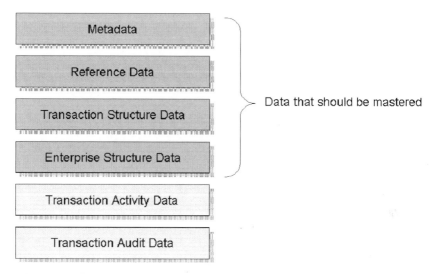

Figure 40.   Master Data

Based on these definitions, it is the author's recommendation that master data is considered to be Metadata, Reference Data, Transaction Structure Data and Enterprise Structure Data (see figure 40).

Levels of Mastering

Master data processes and technologies can be expensive – in terms of resources and time as well as the obvious cost impact. It is therefore important that a sense of proportion in added into the equation. Each master data entity should be graded as regards value to the business and managed accordingly. It is quite possible to have multiple levels of sophistication within the master data capabilities of an organisation from high tech to no management at all.

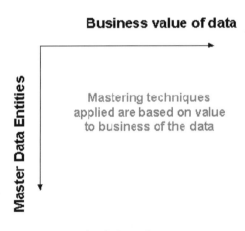

Business value of data

Master Data Entities

Mastering techniques applied are based on value to business of the data

Figure 41.   Levels of Mastering

For example, we would typically expect our customer contact details to be of high value to the business. Customers are no good if we can't contact them to sell more goods. The actual order history of the customer although important is not as important as the customer name, address and phone number. Therefore it would be expected that more resources should be allocated to the customer details than the customer's order history.

Data Residency

When we refer to residency we are looking for the answers to two simple questions:

- Which systems have this data residing in their databases?
- Which system masters this data, by this we mean our 'one true source' of data. It may be that this data isn't mastered by any one system. It is important if we are going to govern data efficiently to at least know where we stand.

Figure 42.   Data Residency Example

	Customer	Product	Order	Account
ERP system	R	M	M	R
Accounting system	R	R	R	M
CRM system	M	R	R	R
Inventory system	R	R	R	R

Key: 'M' = Mastered, 'R' = Resident

The above example maps residency to a set of conceptual data entity for a given set of systems. The level of granularity this analysis is taken to, is dependent on availability of time and resources.

A final comment

So where does the enterprise data model fit with all of this I hear you ask? The enterprise data model is the foundation that MDM is based around. Without the model it is impossible to manage this process effectively. The enterprise data model encapsulates the business and technical understanding of the enterprises core data.

Summary

Within this chapter we have learnt about the different types of data such as Metadata and Transaction Structure Data. A definition for master data is developed and we also touched upon the subject of levels of mastering that will effect business resource allocation to data.

9. Data Governance

This section doesn't intend to define a rigorous process for data governance; as it is the belief of the author that a process should be specific to any given organisation. Instead we address the question of how to use the Enterprise Data Model framework, discussed in this book, to assist a data governance process?

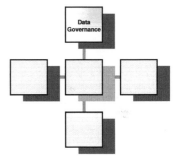

What is Data Governance?

All successful organisations need the individuals within to pull together to achieve objectives. If an organisation grows too large or too complex this becomes difficult to achieve effectively. Governance is an effective mechanism for facilitating this. It is the process through which groups make decisions that direct their collective efforts.

Governance relates to consistent management, cohesive policies, processes and decision-rights for a given area of responsibility. For example, managing at a corporate level might involve evolving policies on privacy, on internal investment, and on the use of data. Good governance stems from—and influences—the core values of the organisation.

Data governance is in reality an assurance process for data. It allows us to add rigor and discipline to managing, using, improving and protecting our organisations data assets. If implemented correctly it can enhance the quality, integration and availability of data by allowing a greater degree of data harmony across the organisation. If implemented badly, it creates a bureaucratic nightmare of standards and red tape.

Data governance:

- Is a set of polices, rules, guidelines and standards for managing data.
- Provides a framework for IT and the business to work harmoniously together to establish common understanding, confidence and credibility in the organisations enterprise data assets.
- Is owned and implemented via a join IT and business team.
- MUST have senior (executive level) sponsorship to succeed.

Governance and the Enterprise Model

So the question still remains as to how we use the Enterprise Data Model framework to assist a data governance process? There are a number of approaches we could use:

- Option 1 would be to use the model as a kind of data definition library that people can pick and choose from as required. Although this approach would provide some value to the organisation, the proposition is not very strong. This option doesn't really seem to me to provide the level of return on the investment in building the model in the first place.
- Option 2 would be to use the enterprise data model as a framework to govern data design across the whole organisation. This would provide a great degree of value add.

Before continuing, a distinction needs to be made between enterprise and project level data models. This separation will allow us to understand the division in responsibility between project and enterprise models. A project data model would typically include a logical data model, as well as a physical data model. An enterprise model would also contain a logical model, but has no physical model as it is not directly implemented.

Figure 43.   *An Enterprise Data Framework*

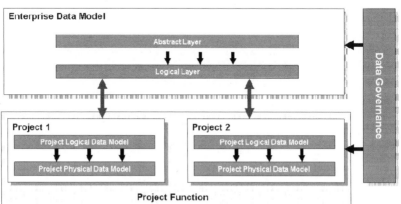

In the diagram above we can see that we have a logical model in both the project and enterprise boxes. The project level logical model will be derived from our enterprise logical model. This creates consistency of data definition; across individual projects and the organisation as a whole. The data governance process is bi-directional (hence the arrow to both project and enterprise level models). A project may provide feedback and refinements to the enterprise model in either the logical or abstract layers.

The enterprise data model acts as a template for projects allowing a rapid progression through the design stages.

Basically the responsibility for the logical data model has been split into an enterprise layer and a project layer. The table below provides some examples of the differences in responsibilities between an enterprise and project level logical data models.

Figure 44.   *Comparison of enterprise and project model responsibilities*

Data Model Activity	Enterprise Logical Data Model	Project Level Logical Data Model
Business definitions of data	Yes	No*
Data model naming standards	Yes	Yes
History (How the application manages historical data)	No	Yes

Non enterprise data required just for individual project eg audit trail of user activity, data driven security etc	No	Yes
Entity and Attribute definitions (eg description, high level data type and valid values for lookups where known.)	Yes	No*

* *Refinements from the enterprise level model based on project specific requirements are included at the project level. This typically will include aspects of the data that do not have any enterprise importance. For example, within the enterprise model we will define the product entity but at the project level we may have an extra attribute called product segmentation category. These attributes are only of interest to marketing, and only exists in the marketing database. The moment the data is needed for more than one application, it starts to have importance at the enterprise level and should be treated accordingly.*

Governance without the stick

Now that the organisation has an enterprise data model, it provides the company with a seismic shift in data governance capability. The model acts as a template for projects, allowing a rapid progression through the design stages. By this I mean that each project team will use the enterprise data model as a starting point for their design. Allowing them to concentrate on the application specific areas of the design rather than trying to redefine (for the 100 time) what is a customer or product etc. This rapid design is achieved without compromising any data standards; in fact we are likely to see a great adherence to data standards. In essence the data governance process can quickly move from a big stick scenario to one of guidance and assistance.

Let's assume, for example, that our enterprise data model has defined the entity product. Within our enterprise definition of product we have (at the logical level) 4 attributes: Product Name, Product Reference Number, Product Weight, and Product Strength. Within the sales and marketing department we have a new campaign management system being developed. This new system requires product data but also needs a new attribute called 'Key Product Indicator'. This attribute allows our sales and marketing teams to know that this particular product is where we should be focusing resources.

At the beginning of the project, the team will be provided with the product definition from the enterprise logical data model. This will leave the design team with only one new attribute to work on; radically reducing the design, build and test effort. Not only do we reduce the effort and costs associated with the project but also the risk.

Outsourcing and Data Governance

It's common in today's globalised world for an organisation to have outsourced project development activities. This is typically done from a financial perspective as massive cost saving can be achieved if the outsourcing model is managed effectively.

The humble data model can play a part in achieving these targeted savings, by introducing a data architecture framework in which the outsourced development process can work. In essence by replacing in figure 43 the 'Project Function' with 'Service Supplier', we can instil adherence to our enterprise data model whilst gaining the advantages of the outsourcing model.

There are a number of challenges that exist with the outsourcing scenario:

- Firstly, you have communication between supplier and customer. Any external supplier will struggle to get up to speed with business terminology associated with the data. An enterprise data model provides definitions and structure to allow clearer understanding of the organisations data. It's hard enough discussing with external consultants, but when you add language and cultural differences it can be like communicating through soup.

- The second issue is the supplier's adherence to customer data standards. Not only does the supplier need to understand and implement them, but this needs to occur without destroying the cost advantage of outsourcing. Providing an enterprise model that vendors can start any project development from, will improve adherence to standards whilst also providing guidance on how to use corporate standards.

- Thirdly, organisations loose knowledge when they employ externals to develop applications for them. The enterprise data model allows the retention of knowledge by capturing definition and understanding from all the key organisational systems and ensuring adherence to common patterns for solving problems.

By using this framework to govern outsourced work you gain the best of both worlds. The client organisation is allowed to focus on the higher level design and architecture aspects, the intellectual property part of the system. The outsourcing vendor is allowed to focus on pure delivery within the logical design framework.

Communication Strategy

Drawing up a communications strategy is an art, not a science. The ability to communicate is essential to the success of data architecture. There are many ways of approaching this task which are dependent on the cultural nuances of the individual organisation. The key point to take on board is that communication does not just happen. It must be organised, developed, and built. The first step in the process is to define a communications strategy.

Summary

This chapter has looked at the impact an enterprise data model can have on an organisations data governance processes. We have seen how our framework can allow a move away from a big stick approach to governance. We can now provide a gear change in the delivery of data projects by providing many parts of the data architecture pre-built. This approach will both reduce risk and cost.

10. Build the Model one Project at a time

Building an enterprise data model is not a new concept. It has been around for years but is often considered as impossible. When I talk about this subject on courses and at conferences I often use a film clip from the 70's series 'Mission Impossible' to emphasise this.

The previous sections have covered the whys and wherefores of data modelling and a framework for enterprise data. This is all well and good but when we put all of this into the context of the real world, we hit the brick wall of practicalities. How on earth can we actually build our enterprise data model? Do we spend 5 years to develop an all-encompassing data architecture or give each project a mandate to work in isolation? In essence how do we actually build and use this framework in a real business environment?

There are three basic approaches to this problem but only one sensible answer. This view has been crystallised within the authors mind after many years of experience, trying out all the options below and collecting, in the process, all the scares to prove it. In summary the options boil down to:

- **Option 1 -** Think Global, Act Global - develop a fully defined abstract and logical layer for the whole enterprise.
- **Option 2 -** Think Local, Act Local – develop individual data models for each project without being hampered by the need to keep consistent with an enterprise level version.
- **Option 3 -** Think Global, Act Local - develop the abstract layer first and then use this as a framework for the development of the logical layer via projects.

To understand what these option mean for your organisation I have explored below each approach in greater detail.

Think Global, Act Global

This approach looks to create the perfect enterprise level data model for your whole organisation. All entities understood, defined consistently and fully documented across the whole organisation.

This was quite common as an approach in the 90's but has proven to be a disastrous experience for most organisations that went and took that route. It is of no value to anyone if a team of data architects commence a 5 year project to map all the data across a global corporation. This type of project would result in a data model that is:

- Out of date and stagnant
- Not understood or supported by the business

- Hugely expensive
- Of no intrinsic value to the business
- An academic work that destroys the organisations confidence in the data architect team as they will be seen as a bunch of ivory tower types.

I have seen a number of these initiatives, undertaken by consultants or internal staff over the years, and they generally follow a common path.

- The vision for an enterprise data model is sold to senior management.
- Project initiated and analysis of key business functions commences.
- Steady progress is maintained as key business entities are identified and defined.
- As detail is developed across the piece many duplications, inconsistencies and oddities are identified in the data.
- Endless cycles of analysis and design ensue, but with little obvious progress. New requirements are found at nearly every business user meeting and it is becoming a political nightmare to agree definitions for detail aspects of the model.
- Questions are asked about the cost of the project and eventually the budget gets cut.
- Project limps onward with a growing sense of negativity from outside and a slowly gathering loss of morale internally.
- Project gets cancelled or mutates into a limited scope tactical project to try and save face.

In essence this approach will typically result in a 'death by a thousand cuts' scenario. It becomes a waste of time, money and generally a very painful experience. It should be noted that there are still a number of 'experts' that advise this route … so be aware!

Think Local, Act Local

A completely project focused approach can seem deceptively tempting. As each project has no ties to any enterprise level governance framework for data, projects can be delivered as required with no delays. This is great for any project focused folk, but should send shivers down the spine of those with an enterprise perspective. In essence, we don't ever arrive at an enterprise model with this approach.

Back in chapter 3 we looked at the example of Widget Ltd who had developed a number of discrete ERP systems. This is in essence the approach Widget Ltd had been using for years and look where it has got them. There are real costs and business flexibility issues associated with this type of approach which are not immediately apparent; but they are painful in the extreme when they do eventually manifest themselves.

Difficulties can be experienced in communicating data concepts with the business due to varying definitions. It is typical that different functions within the organisation will define the same data in differing ways. It therefore follows that the way we structure that data will be inconsistent across projects. Add into this the typical outsource model, with an outsource provider from abroad where English (or whatever language you speak) isn't a first language. Clearly we will find ourselves struggling to re-explain what we now mean when referring to some of the more complex data definitions.

Common definitions for data reduce integration costs between systems. Having an enterprise definition for Customer, for example, will reduce the integration between systems in terms of analysis, design and implementation effort. Not only will it reduce the cost but the risk involved in integration will become more manageable as there are less unknowns.

Chapter 3 covers these issues in greater detail.

Think Global, Act Local

Experience has taught me that it is a combination of both these approaches that is required. We need to have a big picture vision for data whilst at the same time delivering value to the business on a project by project basis.

The Approach

In essence we have a three stage process to move from ground zero, where we have nothing, to an evolving enterprise data model. Notice the use of the word evolving. The enterprise data model will always be in a state of flux as it represents the business. Businesses are prone to mutating over time into different strategic directions with different data requirements.

Step 1 – Develop a first pass model

Develop a first pass abstract model for the whole enterprise. This exercise should be time boxed as a few weeks or months. Clearly the resulting model will be subject to change and improvement over time. The overriding intention is to create artefacts that can guide the development, going forward, of projects that have a data component. From this model we would expect to identify the key data entities, their definitions and the business owners of these data entities. You need at least a conceptual data model, but depending on time and resource availability the creation of a first pass information model. The more complete the greater degree of understanding of the business impact and needs will be gained.

Think Global, Act Local; develop the abstract layer first and then use this as a framework for the development of the logical layer.

Step 2 – work with project teams

Next, as each new IT project starts, the enterprise data architect function can work with the project team; using the conceptual data model as a framework for any logical data model designs. This will obviously need executive support to push through.

Step 3 – evolve the enterprise model

Over time, an enterprise logical data model will be developed that has piggybacked on individual projects. This means that the enterprise data model will move from an artefact in design, to an artefact that can drive data governance. This typically happens almost immediately after the initial project exists its design phase.

The Enterprise Data Model becomes a template for projects.

Because we have mapped out the key data entities across the enterprise, we are able on each project to consider the impact that say 'Product data' may have, to different areas of the business. This is because we already have a reasonably good idea of the data interdependences across the whole organisation not just for our individual project.

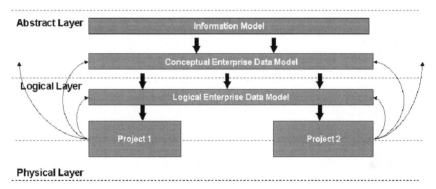

Figure 45.　　*Think Global, Act Local Approach*

The diagram in figure 45 shows the scenario that will come to fruition after only a few iterations. At the bottom, we have two projects that are shown crossing the line between the logical and physical layer; this is because they will contain both logical and physical data models. Both projects are shown, using the enterprise logical data model to provide a template and data governance for their design. After each project, the logical and conceptual models are updated to reflect any areas within those models that need refinement. This can be extended quite naturally to the information model if required.

It should be obvious that we now require:

- A debrief by the data architecture function after each project. This debrief provides an opportunity to review the current data architecture artefacts for areas that need enhancing.
- Data architecture involvement in ALL data related projects. This involvement will be at least in the form of a governance role; to ensure that the framework defined by the Enterprise Data Model is adhered too.

In essence, we are now able to gain all the benefits of an enterprise data model, although admittedly the value will grow over time rather than become 100% recognisable immediately. We have dramatically reduced the costs involved by spreading them throughout all our data related projects under the umbrella role of 'data governance'. Into the bargain we have reduced the risk and costs associated with each new project, after the first, by an increasing factor.

The triangle of constraint

All projects require the management of a triad of pressures – cost, time and quality. This is illustrated in figure 46 below.

The importance of this triangle is that you can not change any one aspect, without effecting at least one of the others. For example, to reduce the time a piece of work takes to deliver you may need to increase the resources allocated to the work (therefore increasing the cost). You might instead reduce the quality of the deliverable rather than impact the cost.

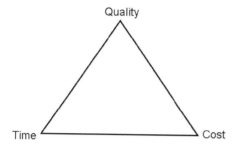

Figure 46.   *Triangle of Constraint*

The reason for including this section is to remind the reader that there will always be time, quality and cost considerations when developing an enterprise data model.

Summary

This chapter has shown how it is possible to build an enterprise data model without spending many years developing it. We have explored an approach to developing such a model that slowly builds knowledge of the enterprises data, project by project, whilst keeping the enterprise cohesion of the data. This approach allows the development of the enterprise data model in phases that relate to the organisations current business imperatives.

11. The Enterprise Data Framework

This is the final chapter of this book and as such it falls upon it to summarise and conclude on the enterprise data model concept.

Data models have been used for decades to model data for specific projects or departments. Although the concept is familiar to most of us, it is still not widely used beyond a purely physical representation of a database. This book uses an enterprise version of the data model to address the challenges facing organisations such as:

- How do we provide a framework within which we can manage our data assets?
- How do we develop applications that adhere to a set of data standards; without creating a nightmare of administration and governance that is both unwieldy and unusable?
- How can we get business value from our enterprise data?

Data is becoming as plentiful as water, although as discussed in chapter 1 that doesn't equate to accessibility. Data like water can be a nightmare to use and understand. Large data volumes bring with them usability, design and technology challenges. Although we have huge volumes of data, only a small percentage is fully understood, of good quality and accessible.

We have defined a few key terms such as data and enterprise data. Data is individual facts that have a specific meaning for a given time period. Enterprise data is data that is of an enterprise nature. By this we mean used by multiple departments, applications or business functions. The key point is that we would expect to see an enterprise data model only contain data that is of an enterprise nature i.e. 'enterprise data'.

The Framework

The data model framework we have developed, over the course of this book, has evolved from being just project focused to spanning the whole enterprise. It has become the central axis of our data architecture capability, and allows successful governance of projects so that data can be managed at an enterprise level rather than in individual project silos. Figure 47 below provides a diagrammatic representation of our final data architecture framework, based on this enterprise data model concept.

At the top of the framework we have the standard capabilities you would expect within a data architecture function; such as data governance, data flows, ownership etc. These capabilities interact through the enterprise model with each other, and interact with data related projects via the same data model backbone.

We have developed a series of layers that decompose the meaning of data at differing levels of abstraction. We start with the business understanding of data (the abstract layer). This is complemented by an information model which allows us to understand the information landscape that the data underpins. We then progress to a business and IT layer (the logical layer), which allows us to fully understand the data structures needed to represent the enterprise aspects of data.

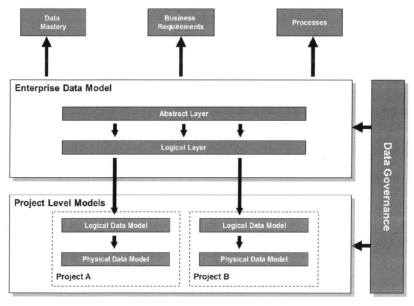

Figure 47.   *The Enterprise Data Architecture Framework*

At the bottom we have the various projects that are impacted by the framework. The logical layer within the enterprise data model provides both governance and guidance as definitions and template models are available rather than just a big governance stick.

In essence we now have a framework that can be used to frame all data related issues, problems and challenges for the business from a strategic to an operational level. To reinforce this concept we will re-look at the Widget example given in chapter 3.

To drive Widget Ltd's consolidation of its manufacturing processes, it is necessary to standardise the usage of product data across the organisation. Currently each ERP system has conflicting data structures, definitions and therefore it becomes impossible to consolidate the data.

The identified differences between just the US and UK ERP systems definitions for product can be summarised as:

- The brand structures and therefore the data held about brand are different. This means Widget's marketing teams can not compare global or similar brands.
- The definitions of Product Name differ between Europe and the US. One is the specific product labelling and the other is just a generic name.
- Product Reference Number and Product Code are not exactly the same piece of data; one is an internal system code whilst the other is a business reference number.
- The US Product Outer Quantity has no equivalent in Europe.

These differences, as we have concluded earlier, result in reducing the company's ability to globalise the product range. The enterprise data model acts as a framework within which to understand and control the data transformation programme that ensues. At the end of the process we have a fully defined and understood product data that is consistent across the organisation. For example Widget now has:

- An abstract layer definition which contains both a conceptual data entity for product and a matching information entity so that the uses of product data and its role in the organisation can be fully appreciated.

- At the logical level we will have a fully understood and defined data structure for product. This will be for both transactional (OLTP) and analytical systems. Within the analytical definition we could have a fully defined product dimension that can be reused across all future data warehouse/mart projects. Future projects will be quicker, contain less technology risk and in general will become more of a component construction activity.
- Data governance processes and standards will be understood, documented and enforced by not only IT, but by the business owners of product data.
- The business usage and value of product data is understood. This means the company can now understand impacts and risks associated with product data changes.
- We understand how product data travels around the various functions of the business.
- And finally we have a clear understand of which systems masters our product data and which don't.

Any changes to product data or technology/processes that manage product data can be fully understood in terms of risk and impact to the business. We also now have a way of insuring the company never returns to the bad old days of data inconsistency.

Maturity Model

There are a wide variety of maturity models out there in the IT world. I don't intend to provide (at this time) another one, I just want to give some sense of the concept.

Typically maturity can be defined in four stages. If we adapt this to the enterprise data model framework, we get the four stages shown in the table below.

Maturity Stage	Description
Leading Light	These organisations have developed a strategy for data and are well down the road of implementing it.
Developed	Has a strategy for enterprise data that is started to be rolled out.
Developing	Developing enterprise data understanding and ability
Not Aware	Not enterprise data aware

Figure 48.   Maturity Model

So why measure maturity?

We measure the organisations maturity not as a pat on the back or some kind of academic exercise, but to allow us to identify areas that need improving.

Some closing points

In closing there are a few points worth bearing in mind.

Free Downloads

There are a few, hopefully useful utilities, which can be down loaded for free on the following website: www.koios-associates.com/edmdownload.htm.

Software Tools

Many people believe that buying the right tool will solve their data problem. Tools don't build data architectures, people do. It takes people to agree definitions with other people and to interpret the complexities in the way that data is structured and understood. A tool supports these people not replaces them. The knowledge and experience you need is tied up in your companies' human capital, not in a tool. There is a phrase used in the UK (not sure how well this translates internationally) – *'don't be a tool'*. In this context a tool can be defined as *'an idiot, a contemptible person'*.

Tools don't build data architectures, people do.

Slow is Faster

By this I mean that you don't have to dive into an all-encompassing initiative to transform the whole organisation within the next 6 months. Instead my advice would be to bite off small chunks of the organisation, so that a steady success wave builds.

It is important with an initiative of this kind to have strong business support. It is the role of the Data Architecture team to help the business understand the importance of managing in a consistent and coherent way the organisations data assets. To succeed this approach requires a shared vision for data that needs executive support as well as architectural vision and control. It requires a partnership between all aspects of the organisation. Companies that manage to make data a key imperative and treat their data asset with correct degree of professionalism, will succeed in the world. Those that don't .... well that's a more complex story.

Appendix A - Enraged Cow Injures Farmer with Axe

This appendix is a light hearted way to demonstrate the power of a diagram in clarifying understanding. It originally comes from a talk I gave to the UK Pensions Regulatory many years ago, and still does the job brilliantly.

During this talk, I went through a series of newspaper headlines that had multiple meaning - some of which are mentioned in chapter 3. To demonstrate the point further, I focused on one specific headline 'Enraged Cow Injures Farmer with Axe' and produced 2 diagrams.

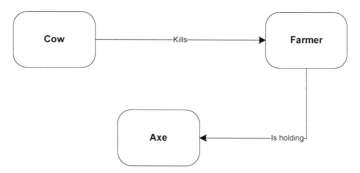

Figure 49.   *Enraged Cow Injures Farmer with Axe – version 1*

Figure 49 above shows that the farmer has the axe but is killed by the cow. Figure 50 shows the poor farmer is killed, but this time by a cow using an axe.

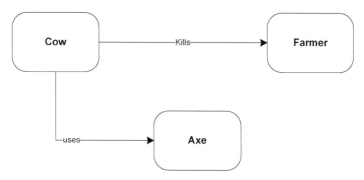

Figure 50.   *Enraged Cow Injures Farmer with Axe – version 2*

These examples don't adhere to any particular notation. They are really just a bit of fun but clearly show the differences between the two versions of the same headline.

Appendix B – Key Points

1 – Introduction

- Data, Data everywhere, nor any information to use
- In essence it allows us to interpret, in diagrammatical form, the business meaning of data in a way that can be consumed by both the business and IT folk.

2 – Information and Data

- Data is individual facts that have a specific meaning for a given time period. Information is data that has context.
- An Enterprise Data Model promotes commonality, reduces risks and improves the quality of data.

3- Pillars of Value

- The enterprise data model can be used, as part of a framework, to understand and manage this fragmented data and instil order and control.
- One of the key foundations stones of MDM is an enterprise data model to govern the use and structure of the organisations data.

- 'Ambiguous' - typically refers to an unclear choice between different definitions as may be found in a dictionary. A sentence may be ambiguous due to different ways of parsing the same sequence of words.
- Increased standardisation and improved clarity of definitions will over time improve the quality of IT systems.
- By making all software adhere to the enterprise data model, the business protects it's self from the impact of changes in technology.
- An enterprise data model improves data quality.

4 – An overview of Data Modelling

- An entity is something about which data will be stored within the system under consideration.
- The relationship is the association between two entities to which all of the occurrences of those entities must conform.
- Normalise to reduce data redundancy or de-normalise to improve performance.
- Standards aid understanding, improve quality and reduce risk.

5 – Enterprise Data Architecture

- Data architecture looks to understand the data structures of the business.
- Most of a companies' data will be held in legacy systems …

6 – The Enterprise Data Model

- An information model is a technique for modelling the abstract business information needs and concepts.

- Conceptual models are used to understand the high level data entities for the domain in question.
- A logical data model is a decomposition of the conceptual data model.
- Physical data models are used to design the actual schema of a database, depicting the data tables, the data columns of those tables, and the relationships between the tables.

8 – Master Your Data

- The enterprise data model is the foundation that MDM is built upon.

9 – Data Governance

- The enterprise data model acts as a template for projects allowing a rapid progression through the design stages.

10 – Build the model one project at a time

- "Think Global, Act Local"; develop the abstract layer first and then use this as a framework for the development of the logical layer.
- The Enterprise Data Model becomes a template for projects.

11 – The Enterprise Data Framework

- Tools don't build data architectures, people do.

References

[1] Edgar Cayce reading reference 5748-5. This psychic reading was given by Edgar Cayce at his home on Arctic Crescent, Virginia Beach, Va., on the 30th of June, 1932.

The reading relates to the mythical library buried under the Great Sphinx of Giza called the 'Hall of Records'. This library is rumoured to house the knowledge of the Egyptians. To date there is no evidence to indicate that the Hall actually exists at all.

[2] Dr. Peter Pin-Shan Chen was a professor of Computer Science at Louisiana State University, who is known for the development of Entity-Relationship Modelling in 1976.

[3] Bachman diagrams are used to design the data using a network or relational "logical" model, separating the data model from the way the data is stored in the system. The model is named after database pioneer Charles Bachman, and mostly used in computer software design.

[4] This quote comes from the film Star Trek II: the Wrath of Khan but there seems to be a few variations in my research on

what the actual quote is. The options seem to be between the following:

- Option 1:
- "Don't grieve, Admiral. It is logical. The needs of the many outweigh..." -- Spock
- "...the needs of the few..." -- Kirk
- "...Or the one." – Spock
- Option 2:
- "In any case, were I to invoke logic, logic clearly dictates that the needs of the many outweigh the needs of the few." – Spock
- "Or the one." -- Kirk

[5] Intangibles: Management, Measurement, and Reporting by Baruch Lev, ISBN-10: 0815700938, ISBN-13: 978-0815700937

[6] The map of the silk road used in this book was copied from the Imperial Tours web site. The URL is:

http://www.imperialtours.net/silk_road.htm.

[7] Between 399 and 414 BC, the Chinese monk Faxian (Fa-Hsien, Fa Hien) undertook a trip via Central Asia to India seeking better copies of Buddhist books than were currently available in China. Although cryptic to the extent that we cannot always be sure where he was, his account does provide interesting information on the conditions of travel along the Silk Road.

[8] Slight exaggeration as there is some evidence of limited contact between China and Rome.

Glossary

Attribute

Each entity has a number of more granular details defined for it such as the model of car, registration number, date of manufacture, colour etc. These detailed pieces of data are called attributes. (See entity)

Canonical Model

A canonical data model is an application independent model that allows application to produce and consume messages in a common format.

Conceptual Data Model

This high-level data model is equivalent to an architect's sketch plan. It is typically used to explore domain concepts with project stakeholders and to provide a framework for further analysis.

Data

Data is individual facts that have a specific meaning for a given time period.

Data Architecture

Data Architecture describes how data is processed, stored, and used by (and between) systems. Data architecture allows the organisation to understand the enterprise data and how this data meet its current and future business strategy.

Data Governance

Enterprise data governance can be thought off as an assurance process for the data.

De-Normalisation

A de-normalised database structure is one that has been specifically designed with performance as its key technical requirement.

Dimension

A de-normalised data structure (see de-normalisation above) used within star and snowflake schemas for performance purposes.

Enterprise

An enterprise is an organisation with a high degree of complexity. Typical examples would include:

- Public sector organisations
- Businesses or corporations
- Joint ventures or partnership

Enterprise Data

Enterprise data is data (see definition for data above) that has a value across the organisation.

Entity

An entity represents a collection of similar objects such as people, places, things, events, or concepts. Examples of entities in an order entry system would include *Customer*, *Address*, *Order*, *Item*, and *Tax*.

Information

Information can be defined as data that has been collected together to create some type of larger context that the individual pieces of data provide

Information Model

Within enterprise data architecture, an information model is a technique for modeling the abstract business information needs and concepts of the organisation under consideration.

Logical Data Model

A logical data model is a lower level of data model than a conceptual model. It should always be technology neutral in design as it is looking to understand the complexities of the data not the technology.

Master Data Management

A methodology focused on providing and maintaining a consistent view of an organisations core business data and its associated definitions. This data is normally dispersed across the organisations. Often called MDM.

Normalisation

Data normalisation is a process in which data is structured so as to reduce and even eliminate data redundancy.

Physical Data Model

Physical data models are used to design the actual schema of a database, depicting the data tables, the data columns of those tables, and the relationships between the tables. This means that the design is based on the technical constraints of the technology platform.

Star or Snowflake schema (see de-normalisation)

A database design approach that is typical when de-normalising a database.

XSD

An XSD is the definition document for your XML. Before you process an XML file you ensure it is in the right format you validate it against an XSD file. The XSD defined the valid structure that your application can process.

Training

At Koios Associates we run a variety of training programs to support the development of the data architecture professional. To find out more please check out the latest courses and course schedule from our website: www.koios-associates.com.

Index

Index

2726500R00085

Printed in Great Britain
by Amazon.co.uk, Ltd.,
Marston Gate.